More than Enough

Discover Your Limitless Potential and Live Your Bravest Dream

May you always live your bravest dream —
Lara Jaye

LARA JAYE

Dedication

I would like to dedicate this book to my sons, Daniel and Tyler. Without your love, encouragement, and support this book would have never been written. Thank you for making me smile, even on the darkest days. Love you both very much!

Raving Reviews

"Thoughtfully Written for Our Busy World!"

"I found this to be an easy read... thoughtfully written for our busy world and purely shared as the truths of your precious heart. You are so loved and admired. Your story will help shape stronger lives... even SAVE lives. Your authentic life will continue to bless others abundantly. God is using you daily in a mighty and deep way. I was blessed immensely from your spirit-led book with God's seal of approval! Many things you shared resonated with me and I am applying your noted healing and growing methods."

— Stacy Paetz

"Identified with Every Piece of This Book!"

"Thank you for writing this book. And just Thank GOD for you. I laughed, I cried, I identified with every piece of this book and it touched my soul. If I could have written a book (I always wanted to) - this is what I would have written. So again, THANK YOU! I'm always relieved to know there is someone else going through the same things and even more so when it is things that are so very similar. I'm also relieved to know that I am handling situations 'properly' or attempting to go down the right path. But I also know that I still have work to do. We have many obstacles to overcome. This book has given me a spark again to keep moving forward towards knowing that I/we are enough where we are."

— Jennie Boller

"I Started Reading and Could Not Stop!"

"I started reading and could not stop. More Than Enough allows the reader to connect with the author and clients in the book. This book allows the reader to be guided on how to feel ENOUGH without being judgmental or all-knowing. Clearly written by someone who truly knows how hard it is to move from the past to the present. Wow. A must for my library. I will be referring regularly to ENOUGH as I continue on my journey of learning to know I am ENOUGH."

— Kenda Hamersley, Mom, Grandmother, and Teacher

"Thoughtfully Laid Out and Easy to Understand!"

"It is very clear that Lara is someone who practices what she teaches in More Than Enough. The book is thoughtfully laid out and easy to understand. If I could only choose one chapter from this book to share with everyone, my pick would be Chapter 3 because there is nothing better, in my opinion, than experiencing 'being fully present, here and now.' Thank you, Lara, for the privilege of reading your work before its release, it was a true pleasure!"

— Shelly Allen, Master Empowerment Coach, ShellyAllen.com

"Generous Steps are Easy to Follow!"

"Your loving and generous steps are easy to follow, and will be helpful to those seeking a path to find inner peace through self- love, on their journey to realizing that they too... are ENOUGH."

— Glenda Meyer

"A Must Read for Anyone Seeking More Satisfaction!"

"More Than Enough is a must read for anyone seeking more satisfaction and peace in their everyday life! Lara's profound spiritual journey and real world stories will make you cry and then make your heart soar. I found myself nodding in agreement as she described parts of her life before Limitless Soul. With the steps she outlines in each easily digestible chapter, you will be well on your way to loving yourself, and discovering your soul's purpose. I enjoyed every minute of this relatable read, and I can't wait for the next one!"

— Lacey Ring-Verbik, Imagine Virtual Assistant Service

"I Realize How Important it is to Take Care of Myself!"

"I now realize how important it is for me to take care of myself. I neglect myself when it comes to eating right and exercising. I need to be 'quiet'; my busy brain can take over which greatly diminishes my quality of rest/sleep. It is okay and essential to take care of myself! Eat, sleep, and exercise for a new me!"

— Julie Meyer

"Renewal of Self-Acceptance for Me!"

"I started your book and could not put it down—awesome work filled with good methods and personal examples. Loved the chapter setup with summaries. I walked on air for several days and can still evoke that feeling by thinking of your book. I needed to renew myself and your book was right on time. I'm blessed to read it as a draft. So exhilarating! Renewal of self-acceptance for me. Bless you for sharing. Perfect chapter summaries to lead the way to enough."

— Rita J. Rose

"A Necessity for Health, Happiness and Fulfillment!"

"As I read More Than Enough, I was struck by how many of the daily destroyers of 'self- love' applied to my life... and how I perceived my value. I have been known to apologize profusely and assume responsibility for things that weren't my fault, because as Lara states in the book, 'I was merciless with myself.' Additionally, I would put my needs last, because I didn't want to let down anyone who requested my assistance. After all, there would be time for me to engage in personal resilience later, right? More Than Enough is a 'must read' and important in understanding that 'self love' is not a luxury... but, a necessity for health, happiness and fulfillment!"

— Mary Burkhart

"I Accepted Your Challenge!"

"I, too, did not think I was GOOD ENOUGH most of my life. I accepted your challenge about walking 15 minutes, outside, every day. At first, I didn't think it would make that much of a difference. Boy, was I wrong! Your book has made me realize that I need to set boundaries in my life and that it's okay to say NO to people. My girls are grown with their own families. It's time for me! It's time to live my life for me!"

— Cindy Wood

"I Love the useful, practical advice!"

"I love the useful, practical advice. Lara does not take a 'one size fits all' approach. She celebrates that individuals have to use the approach that works best in their life. She skillfully combines that with specific suggestions anyone can use."

— Lisa Dumeyer

"This Book Resonated with Me!"

"Many principles of this book resonated with me – self-love, the importance of nutrition and exercise, recognizing and committing to priorities, setting boundaries, asking for help, meditation and time in nature, etc. Given my finance background, it probably comes as no surprise that I strongly agree with the importance of being aware of your financial situation. Making responsible, sound decisions you can feel good about, not just in the moment, but also long-term plays an enormous role in both mental and physical health."

— Amber Winchester, Finance Professional, Retired at 38

"You Made Me Feel Like it was Okay to Slow Down!"

"You've got a gentle way of saying what so many of us need to hear. As a type-A personality, I'm used to pushing and pushing but when I was finished with the book, I felt like it was okay to slow down and focus on myself, something that society, in general, doesn't value. After all, we're 'human beings, not human-doings.' LOVED that line. Overall, the book is comforting because you share your story. I love hearing stories from fellow human beings, usually because we can all relate to each another that way. Thank you for telling yours."

— Jay Hankins

"An Interesting and Compelling Read!"

"I really enjoyed and appreciated the opportunity to read your manuscript! It was definitely an interesting and compelling read, especially because it was backed by your personal experiences. Your book reminds me a lot of one of my favorites, How to Win Friends and Influence People by Dale Carnegie."

— Ryan Van Slyke

"Motivated Me to Care More for Myself, Without Guilt!

"Lara shared insight regarding the same worries I've kept in the back of my mind for years. Things I've struggled to release. Her positive reminders and support motivated me to care more for myself and love myself, without guilt. Greatly appreciated the 'sparks' and compassion this angel has for those in need."

— **Wendy Crandall**

"A Perfect Blend of Self Help Ideas!"

"More Than Enough is a perfect blend of self-help ideas and interesting autobiography. Although it is best read slowly to focus on each self-care suggestion, the book in its entirety is a very pleasant, easy read. Ideas and suggestions abound in an encouraging, supportive commentary. This is a great go-to book for personal growth and positive affirmation. Best of all, it offers inspiration!"

— **Lorie Dilanchian (Choir Director, Danville Community Schools, Danville, Indiana)**

"Simple and Profound Life Changing Practices!"

"I found Lara's book to be inspiring because it is so real! It's an amazing treasure of seemingly simple but profound and life changing practices that she used to heal herself from the 'I am not enough' syndrome that is so pervasive in our culture. She speaks from her heart and her experience, offering advice we can trust. For me, reading Lara's book was like listening to a dear friend, sharing her wisdom from 'the trenches' of life and showing practical steps to reclaim our self-love as our birthright."

— **Elizabeth Haines, Client Attraction Magic for Healers, Therapists, and Coaches at ehaines.com**

"Great Motivational Book for All Aspects of Your Life!"

"Great motivational book for all aspects of your life. In just three days, it has changed my perspective and made me question what is really important, what can I say no to and how can I take better care of myself. I have already stepped out of my box and feel energized and relaxed."

— LaDonna Sloan

"I Enjoyed Learning Different Ways to Deal With Stress!"

"I enjoyed reading More Than Enough and learning of different ways to deal with stress. I do take advantage of the silence of nature often in my backyard. At church, the Pastor speaks of evil trying to talk you down in your head, and I loved the way you describe it as 'mind chatter.' It is important not to listen to it when the chatter is negative."

— Vicki Jo Lee

"The Truths are Real and Alive Inside Every One of Us!"

"Lara reaches deep inside herself and pulls out the truths the vast majority of people don't like even to think about. The truths are real and alive inside every one of us, and her step-by-step advice can surely lead anyone down a path to recovery from their problems."

— Tyler Habig

"I Really Enjoyed it!"

"Great job! I really enjoyed it! Thank you for sharing your book with us. "

— Valerie V.

"Felt as if I was on The Path of Self-Healing!"

"The moment I began reading Lara Habig's words on clearing my mind of its chatter, and the 'Be Still' concept, I immediately felt as if I was on the path of self-healing. Being shown how to see that I am Enough has given me the courage to take in her most important message, that it is not selfish to take care of myself. I eagerly await a follow-up on this life changing topic of self- love."

— Lauren Beretta, Massage Therapist, Doula, and Energy Worker

"A Book That Every Woman Must Read!"

"More Than Enough is a book that every woman must read, especially in today's society where it's acceptable and sometimes expected for women to play small. If you have ever experienced negative self-talk, indecisive self-doubt, or self-deprecating dialogue, then Lara Habig's powerful yet compassionate voice will certainly help you Discover Your Limitless Potential and Live Your Bravest Dream."

— Lena Anani, Author of OMG Do It Now: Be the Voice You Want to Hear in the World

"I Agree Whole-Heartedly with Lara's Advice!"

"I agree wholeheartedly with Lara's advice when it comes to taking care of ourselves. All too often, we tend to 'outdo' ourselves by over-scheduling our day. I can attest to this because I tend to be 'doing' all the time and forget to schedule time for just ME. I need to consciously force myself to get outside to walk and enjoy nature, while just taking in the moment. I'm going to start setting aside daily time where I can just BE!"

— Rose B., Elementary School Secretary

Contents

Acknowledgements

Dr. Barb Koewler: An understanding and loving friend who has supported me through the unbelievable ups and downs of my life. You remained a good friend even though I fought taking your health advice! For that, I thank you for letting me learn on my own and for not saying "I told you so!" I promise I will listen from now on! Love you!

Andrea Beaman: The short time we worked together was life-changing. Your focus on self-love altered the way I viewed my life. Thank you for blessing me with your gifts. You laid a foundation that cannot be shattered.

Carmina McGee: I am in awe of your extensive knowledge and how it applies to the healing of my body. You have reminded me often that I am in charge of my support team. Thank you for guiding me with love, information, and discernment to make the best decisions for my health and my body.

Lena Anani: My patient and caring book coach who believed in me even when I didn't believe in myself. Thank you for your support and your ability to flow with my crazy life as I was writing this book. You are much appreciated!

Melissa Harnish: You're a dear friend who has stuck with me through good times and bad. We have laughed and cried together, all the while knowing there would be brighter days ahead. Thank you for your non-judgmental and never ending support.

Sonia Barnes: Thank you for your consistent friendship even as my life took many twists and turns. You jumped on my roller coaster ride of a life and kept cheering me on. You are much appreciated and loved! Thank you for being YOU!

Rose Berg: We have spent many days together since first meeting when our children were preschool age. Memories I will cherish forever. Each moment has been peppered with laughter and tears, sometimes fear, but always love. Thank you for being YOU!

To the AUMC Ladies: (Carol, LaDonna, Valerie, Lisa, Penny, Pamela, Vicki, Melissa, Rose, Sonia and Miss Betty) Thank you for your friendship, guidance, and love over the years. You each have a place in my heart that laid the foundation for who I am today.

Dr. Shaun Dumas: You were a Godsend as I struggled to get well last winter. I looked forward to every acupuncture treatment because you gave me hope for wellness. Thank you for being you!

And, of course, to my family: I know you all don't necessarily understand my journey, but you have loved and supported me nonetheless.

Mom and Dad: (Layden and Suzie) Thank you for reminding me to stand up for myself and live my own bravest dream.

Steven: I know you thought you were going to be the big brother in this book, but really, I am thankful you were as hard on me as you were. Through that experience, I am stronger and better able to handle the world as it is. Much love and thanks to you.

Brian: To the brother who is *perfect* in every way or at least, so he reminds me! Thank you for your support and love. You make me smile as I know you always have my back.

Lisa: To my little sister who was spoiled and got everything she wanted! Just kidding, you are amazing, loving, and supportive. Without you and your sweet girls (Kylie and Kaci), there would have been many more sad days. You picked me up when I was down and reminded me to keep going when things got tough. Thank you for being there for me no matter what. You have taught me, by example, true self-love.

Liana Chaouli: Thank you to my mentor at ImageTherapists.com who continued to hold the vision for this book and the work that I do in the world when I couldn't see it myself. She gets up under you "like a boulder" to support and push you to your God-given destination of only the very highest and best. Much heartfelt gratitude to you and your team for not letting me stay small and hide!

And, of course, to all my beautiful friends, family, and mentors not mentioned above: Every one of you has played an important part in my life and the writing of this book. I am forever grateful and honored to be a part of your life – whether it was for a short time or a lifetime. Thank you for loving and supporting me even when I couldn't do it for myself.

How to Read this Book

There are two ways you can read this book. No matter what way works best for you, first read the *Introduction* so you can fully understand the rest of the book. One option is to read straight through. Another option is to read the *Introduction* and then pick ANY chapter that interests you. Re-read that specific chapter for a complete month, working through the questions and challenges I offer. Take your time as you work through each chapter, recording your notes in the back of the book. Read this book as you are led, in order or broken into segments. Regardless of *how* you read it, embrace this book as your guide to a luxurious life of self-love and deep satisfaction!

Introduction

*"Low esteeem is like driving through
life with the hand-brake on."*

— Maxwell Maltz

For many years now I have felt like something deep inside of me was screaming to be heard. On most days, I ignored it. It was easy to dismiss my soul's calling, or so I thought. When my crisis of faith intersected with health issues and a divorce after twenty-five years of marriage, listening to my soul calling became my guiding light on the dark days. That light was my soul, or God spark as I refer to it, crying to be heard.

When I finally began to hear what my soul was trying to tell me, I realized that my past pain and suffering were not in vain. It was a conduit to my soul's calling here on earth. It was guiding me all along to do what I came here to do in this time and place.

What if that is the case with you as well?

What if your pain is your access point to your purpose? What if your suffering is the conduit to *Your Soul's Calling*?

For me, this journey has led me down a road of helping others who believe they are not enough. Depression, anxiety, eating disorders, self-hate, and self-neglect may be ruling your life like it did mine. Questions run through most of our minds, like: Are you thin enough yet? Smart enough? Tall? Pretty? Enough money in your bank account? Are you enough to pursue your dream?

Am I enough? That is what most every person wants to know at their core.

What is it going to take for you to believe you are enough?

Sooner or later it seems we all entertain the idea that we aren't enough. The problem isn't that it only happens once or even twice. It can be so ingrained in our psyche that our self-esteem is annihilated. Like cancer, it can spread quickly and dangerously.

Afflicting most everyone in the world at one time or another, a negative self-image affects our energy and our spirit. Quickly, it can conquer every area of our lives. It can take down a person's whole world. Even entire families and generations. We crave something and look everywhere for it. We become desperate, seeking fulfillment in other people, food, drugs, work, anything and everything, attempting to dull the pain of not enough and never succeeding.

Maybe you're going through a divorce, or maybe you detest yourself. Been there, done that. Sometimes not believing you're enough comes out as anger, depression, lack of self-care, fear, feeling worthless, or people-pleasing. I know exactly how you feel, and lived through it to tell tales. Those days when you loathe yourself so much that you can't get out of bed. Those days when you cry yourself to sleep or can't look at yourself in the mirror.

Self-esteem is confidence and satisfaction in yourself. It's also tied to your self-respect. It's how you think and feel about yourself. Your health, relationships, even your job may be affected by the way you value (or don't value) yourself. Self-esteem (or lack of it) can affect every area of your life. It can help you hold your head high and feel proud of yourself and what you do, even when things don't seem to be going well. Self-esteem gives you the courage to try new things and the power to believe in yourself. It's a measure of how you see yourself and how you feel about your life.

I want to make it clear that having self-esteem isn't about bragging! A healthy self-esteem is an inner knowledge that you are worthy exactly as you are. You accept and love yourself at this moment—flaws and all!

If self-esteem is a measure of how you see yourself and how you feel about your life, it will make sense to have good self-esteem; we would need to do things for ourselves and our lives that honor the amazing creations that we each are. Essentially, to have a healthy self-esteem, loving ourselves is a must.

Not loving yourself is like watching dominos fall, one right after the other. Choosing not to eat healthily or exercise will send you down the road of challenging health issues. Choosing to allow anger to overcome you will most likely result in hurting others or, if pushed inward, depression and health issues.

Not loving yourself can also present itself in one or more of these ways where you:

- Get frustrated easily.
- Have an eating disorder.
- Withdraw socially.

- Have an inability to see yourself *squarely* or to be fair to yourself.

- Can't accept compliments.

- Neglect yourself.

- Treat yourself badly, but not other people.

- Are reluctant to take on challenges.

- Can't put yourself first.

- Don't trust your opinion.

- Expect little out of life for yourself.

Folks who struggle with self-love can't believe they are ENOUGH. No matter how hard they try or how often they hear it from others, they can't seem to believe they are good enough.

Self-love is a gentle acceptance, an unconditional sense of support and caring, and a core of compassion for yourself. It is an abiding willingness to meet your needs, allow yourself to feel and think whatever you feel and think, and to see yourself as essentially worthy, good, valuable, and belonging in the world, deserving of happiness. And, most importantly, believing that you are ENOUGH, as you are, at this moment. Self-love is developed early in life, and if childhood experiences damage our sense of self significantly, a lack of self-love can hurt us for a lifetime.

We need to have a healthy self-esteem and practice self-love because it affects every aspect of our lives. It's essential, because:

- Without it, we can crumble and not show up for our life.

- It helps us feel good about ourselves.

- It gives us the courage to try new things.

- It helps us honor and respect ourselves, even when we make mistakes.

- It encourages us to make healthy decisions for our minds and bodies.

All this does not mean that a person with good self-esteem discounts others, but instead they value themselves and ensure their feelings or needs are not discounted.

– My Story –

In the past, I thought it horribly selfish to say I loved myself. I didn't understand people around me who took time out of their days to care for themselves. True self-love isn't greedy, selfish or egoistical, but somehow I learned it was selfish – almost sinful – to take care of myself. I believed it was greedy to take the time to work out or relax. Churches I attended didn't help much either. They are set up to encourage volunteering. Coming from the background I did, I pushed myself by helping others until I was wiped out because that's what I thought I HAD to do.

When I finally got off the hamster wheel of taking care of everyone else but myself, I realized how important and honorable self-love is. I see now that to have a loving relationship with others we must have a loving relationship with ourselves FIRST, and that means practicing self-love! The problem when we don't love ourselves or take care of ourselves is we will not feel good– physically or emotionally. And, when we don't feel good, we can't fully love those around us. We can even be resentful towards others who do honor themselves.

My reality not so long ago was difficulty, depression, anxiety, eating disorders, self-hate, and self-neglect. My low self-confidence would further fuel me into not showing up for ME. Un-kept commitments to myself led me into an even deeper depression. Spiritually and emotionally, I was unfulfilled. Empty.

My early years were filled with stress, unpredictability, and sorrow. As a child, I didn't know how to have fun. I was the overly responsible sibling, always wanting to make sure everyone was happy and their needs were met. Not understanding why I also carried this burden into adulthood. It was peace at all costs. Shame and fear were my constant companions, never allowing me to trust myself or my feelings. Don't talk, don't trust and don't feel were the subconscious messages I would send myself. I tended toward impulsive decisions and couldn't fully share who I was out of fear.

When I was twenty-one years old, I married my hometown boyfriend, who was six years older. He was very predictable and provided a feeling of safety. Both of us were raised in a Protestant, Christian church and cherished our traditional marriage. Before marrying, we agreed on having three or four children. After we had two wonderful boys, he wasn't interested in having additional children. However, I felt strongly in my heart that God was still calling us to have at least one more child. This heartbreak sent me into a deep depression. I began to feel so incomplete; I could barely function on some days.

For years, we tried counseling. However, we could never come to an agreement, or understanding. Counselors called what we were experiencing a *classic gridlock*. They told us we needed to become friends again and start over before we could even discuss the issues with love, empathy, and compassion. That never happened. I felt unheard, unseen, and abandoned. My dream of having additional children solely rested on another human being's choice and it was not to be.

During these difficult years, my health began to decline. Along with the depression, at thirty-nine I had a complete hysterectomy due to endometriosis. Needless to say, I was devastated. Although I was ever so thankful for our two boys I was able to birth, my dream of having additional children was not to happen.

A perceived lack of support in my life made it seem I had nowhere to turn. I was the woman on the sidelines watching life pass by. Strangely enough, from the outside, things were picture perfect... a successful husband, successful home business, beautiful home, two amazing and talented sons, a great school system, fabulous vacations, a tight-knit community, and church family. Every-THING the normal American family desires and more.

But, on the inside, I was dying. Utter despair and depression over-took me. Antidepressants became my safety net to stay in my hollow life. Attempting to dull the pain of not enough, but never succeeding, I knew it wasn't lady-like to be angry at others, so I subconsciously turned my anger inwards. After all, I was a *good* Christian woman, and I loved everyone... everyone except myself. I was merciless with myself.

– Healing Self-Hatred –

Although many negative beliefs were implanted at an early age, as an adult, I believed the lies my mind chatter pounded at me. Lies like: You are fat. You are ugly. You are stupid. God wasn't paying attention when he made you. You are not enough. You have to do more. Be more. You are a mistake. Lies and more lies. I believed them. I didn't know any different. I suspect the early sexual abuse and generations of alcohol addiction played into these beliefs.

To numb myself from the pain that antidepressants couldn't begin to alleviate, I made myself even busier. I taught Bible Studies, attended other Bible Studies, ran a moms' group, volunteered at the kids' schools, worked two part-time jobs including my marketing company, volunteered at the church (Christian education, marketing committee, youth groups), and volunteered for the local education foundation and more. And, frankly, for years I appeared to be very successful at juggling all those balls.

My health continued a downward spiral with what seemed to be no return. Symptoms such as fatigue, anxiety, weight gain, hair loss, puffy face, sweating, difficulty sleeping, irritability, muscle weakness, depression, dry skin, and forgetfulness were beginning to worsen. I was struggling on many days even to get out of bed. I kept telling myself I was just in a funk and needed to get out more!

I made myself busier and busier. None of which seemed to take the pain away, though, of not enough.

I was surrounded by people and things but felt ever so isolated. Exhausted, I was hanging on by an invisible thread. Even with counseling, my marriage was also crumbling at a rapid rate.

Looking back, my entire life has been the ENOUGH message. Like many of us, I never thought I was enough or had enough. I thought that I had to "do-do-do" all the time. Although I felt strongly led by God to have more children, I believed that I HAD to have more children before I was complete. It was a horrible feeling to know your dreams were in someone else's hands and you didn't have any say. Struggling against my circumstances, I became furious at God, my ex-husband and the world as I fought my inner demons of not being enough.

– The Spark Of Hope –

Although it seemed my life was imploding, there was always a small spark inside that kept me going. I knew deep in my soul that there was more to life than this box I had put myself in.

Due to my perplexing health issues, I became desperate for nutrition counseling and was led to a Godly spiritual leader for assistance. What began with nutrition information became a turning point towards a new life of deep satisfaction and complete fulfillment in all areas of my life. In many ways, I knew all along that I desired more of God and thought I could get it at a church. What I realized, though, was that God was inside of me the entire time and I just needed to learn how to listen and trust.

I would remind myself often that my soul was limitless and began to believe that anything was possible. Each day, I would release and reconnect to myself. Daily, I reset to remind myself of the possibilities. Silencing that inner critic was my job 24/7. All the answers of the hard questions began with looking within.

Gradually, each day built upon itself and with each step, I became stronger. When the dark days began to diminish, I could see I was ENOUGH just as I was. Acceptance and love for myself emerged, and with it, dormant healing abilities arose from the ashes of what was my life. Angels appeared and spoke to me. When others needed healing, God would speak through me—usually in a language I didn't understand.

As scared as I was of this newfound treasure, I embraced the new me, allowing God and His angels to work in my life. Not surprisingly, confidence and passion for life returned with a vengeance, and my business Limitless Soul was born!

When I began thinking about loving myself, I couldn't even say the words. I would cringe. Intuitively, I knew that I needed to practice self-love, but I still couldn't say the words. So, instead, I began the practices outlined in this book as a foundation for loving myself, until I could say the words. With each step, I gained confidence in myself and my place in the world. Slowly but surely, the tug o'war I had with my self-hatred continued until gradually it began standing back up on its own.

I learned how to do many of the things I talk about in the following chapters. These seemingly simple practices were the beginning of an entirely new outlook on life for me. I finally came to realize that I was enough just as I am. I no longer had to look outside of my life to know I'm okay. No one else can give you the desires of your heart. The perfect job, life, body, accomplishments, or amount of money in the bank will not EVER be able to tell you and sustain for you that you are enough. There's never enough if you need something outside of yourself. It's only what's going on in your consciousness, your soul that can prevent you from being happy.

This book is for you if you are not sure if you're enough. It will help you realize your true value and encourage you into pursuing your own bravest dreams. It begins with loving yourself. There are many ways to practice self-love, and this book will touch on the main practices I implemented in my life.

You can expect the same results I received when implementing these practices. Results such as:

- Release self-limiting beliefs that hold you back from greatness.

- Release old patterns and open yourself up to unlimited possibilities.

- Reconnect with your soul's desire to enjoy the beauty of life.

- Renew your divine commitment to self-care and self-worth.

- Renew your spiritual connection.

- Renew your commitment to pursuing your greatest dreams.

- You will value and love yourself.

- You will know you are ENOUGH.

- You will have HOPE.

- Become a healthier person — mind, body, and spirit.

- You will learn how to hear from God.

- Fears will fade, and confidence will soar right into your bravest dream.

I am honored and humbled to offer my journey as an example of realizing you are ENOUGH. Consider me your spark of hope tour guide! If you can believe in yourself with the little spark of hope that's left, you can soar into your bravest dream. I can help you see your limitless potential even when you can't see it for yourself. But, most importantly, you will begin to see your past pain and suffering can be the conduit to your greatest gift to the world— Your Soul's Calling. Enjoy!

Now it's your turn

Introduction

You'll want to obtain a notebook or journal to record your thoughts and feelings as you journey to becoming **Enough**. Select one which reflects you and your beautiful personality. Or, pick a plain one you can decorate as you discover yourself in a whole new way.

In your journal as you work your way through More Than Enough, you'll be asked to reflect and jot ideas or thoughts down.

- How did my story sound similar or dissimilar to your own?

- Were there moments were you felt squirmy or uncomfortable?

- What messages run through your mind as if on a tape recording? Do these messages serve you?

Remember, your awakening is a marathon and not a sprint. Spend at least a week in each chapter, reading it several times, reflecting, and working through the Now It's Your Turn sections at each chapter's end.

Be Still

Taking time to do nothing often brings
everything into perspective.

– Doe Zantamata

In today's fast-paced society, the majority of us are on information overload: exhausted, worn out, and depleted. We are tired. Our bodies are screaming for healthy, nutritious food and eight hours of uninterrupted sleep. Our minds are ready to explode from all the information and advertising we take in every day.

We seem to be running around non-stop, sometimes not even sure where we are going! We fill our days with ceaseless electronic communication (internet, TV, video games, cell phones, and movies) and constant driving to/from activities, including take-away meals. Many of my days included picnics in the school parking lot while my boys ate a quick meal before their sport or band practice. We go-go-go. We do-do-do. We put out fires all day long. The urgent tasks seem to scream at us, while the important tasks silently stand nearby waiting patiently.

In our daily lives, many of us even resort to praying on the run, hoping even a smidgen of what we request gets through the busy lines. We ask question after question. We ask for help and wonder why we don't get answers. There is so much noise in our lives we couldn't hear the answers anyhow. Physically, spiritually, many of us are depleted.

That was me. As my body was running on empty, I was forced to *Be* Still.

I encourage you to try it before you are forced! Be Still. Just sit there. Stare out the window at nature as long as you possibly can! Notice how you feel. What does it feel like? How long can you sit still with nothing to do? Time moves slowly at first. Then, you embrace it. You crave the BEING. You look for ways to stop DOING all the time, so there is more time JUST to BE.

With my graphic design background, I naturally look for white space. This white space is the place on the page where your eyes can rest. You can breathe there. I invite you to look for white space in your life. Where can you breathe? If you can't find any room, you need to look even closer and see what needs to go. Natural white space in your day will allow you just to BE.

For me, it looks like quiet mornings with a cup of coffee, enjoying nature. It's my time to regroup and just BE. No hurry. I had to give up my morning rush, though. Rush, rush, rush. Go-go-go. It was exhausting, and I was exhausted.

Last winter the polar vortex swirled around Central Indiana where I live. As the days grew shorter, so did my patience. I would hear God says to me, "*Be Still* and Know." I thought, "I am being still, but I don't KNOW what you are doing!" Soon I realized that I didn't need to know what He was doing. I had to make the concerted effort to *Be Still*. And, honestly, if you can't *Be Still* with yourself and slow down, you can almost guarantee that eventually God will put something in your path to make you still!

I was completely exhausted but continued to press my body and schedule beyond healthy parameters. God was trying to get my attention. Again, I say, if you don't force yourself to slow down, God will! I quit one of my part-time jobs and began hiring help for my marketing company. I cut back on all volunteerism except that which allowed me to be with my two high school-aged boys. The rest of it was out. My friends were curious and rather stunned at what I was doing. Frankly, so was I! But I knew my life depended on it. My marriage needed work, but first I knew I needed to work on me. After that I could assess better if the marriage could continue.

Well-meaning friends would ask me, "What are you doing?" I honestly didn't have an answer. I wasn't doing anything. I was being. By the way, we are not human-doings. We are human-beings. It was the start of something beautiful for me to realize that. I didn't have to *do-do-do* all the time. I could just BE. It was beautiful and freeing!

The pressures of the outside world melted away as I embraced this new way of life. I followed my guidance every moment and got STILL. Being Still for me meant to slow down my life, cut out activities, and at times, sit on the couch and stare out the window like the children in The Cat and The Hat Comes Back!

This simple, deliberate act of Being Still became a daily ritual I relished (and still do). I can't explain it, but in the stillness, I began to:

- Be present.
- Enjoy each moment at a deeper level.
- Feel feelings and release pent up frustrations.

- Reconnect to the God spark inside of myself.

- Have visions of angels.

- Trust and honor myself.

- Know that I am ENOUGH just as I am.

- Feel centered and energized to fulfill my soul's purpose.

- Hear God clearer.

Without being still we stumble through the noise. Without being still we take guesses at where we should be next. Without *being still*, we don't honor ourselves or our true calling.

A few years ago, I switched to wearing silver and white gold jewelry, having shunned my usual gold. In some recent work with a mentor, Liana Chaouli, I put a gold necklace on but it didn't feel right, and I quickly took it off. As I held the necklace, it brought tears to my eyes for no apparent reason and sent me into a tailspin! I began to do what I encourage you to do: sit with it. Let come up whatever needs to come up. I asked myself, what is it about this necklace that was upsetting me? Almost immediately, I realized the gold represented my gold wedding ring and love, which now was gone after the divorce.

As I dug even deeper, the gold necklace reminded me of lost love. Both my parents and grandparents expressed their love for one another through jewelry—normally gold. One Christmas in particular, my Grandfather presented my Grandmother with a beautiful gold brooch of two geese, stating his love for her while making the comparison that geese mate for life. A simple gold necklace changed my life that afternoon. I was able to release the feeling of lost love in my own life by noticing and taking the time to dig into the real meaning of my tears. But first I had to *Be Still* and feel.

If we choose to pay attention to our soul's calling, there will be always be moments such as mine with the gold necklace. These are the moments that stop us in our tracks. We get to decide whether we're going to continue numbing ourselves with more unimportant activities or if we are going to step up and observe what is happening in our lives. As we observe, we can feel the emotions that are attached to various moments, release them, and move on from a stronger point.

We are all so busy in our lives. Too busy, perhaps. When I made the effort to slow down and reevaluate my life, miracles began to arrive by the handful. In the stillness, I became more aware of the unseen world around me. God and His angels were guiding my every step. Every word. Every intention. I felt supported and loved. All of sudden, I had more time for my children. More one-on-one, face-to-face, real talk time to connect with my kids and friends. Meaningful conversations emerged, and not only the to-do list for the day. Peace overflowed out from me as a result of my time of stillness. An inner-knowing blossomed, giving me confidence in my decisions.

Mother Teresa described this quietness well saying:

> *I'm a little pencil in the hand of a writing God, who is sending a love letter to the world. God cannot be found in noise and restlessness. God is the friend of silence. See how nature — trees, flowers, grass — grows in silence; see the stars, the moon and the sun, how they move in silence... We need silence to be able to touch the soul.*

Tiffany began her stillness practice by embarking on a VIP Retreat with me. Fed up with her crazy, busy, out-of-control life, Tiffany hopped on a plane last minute and flew to a beautiful island, where I worked with ladies one-on-one.

Exhausted and depleted, she had been working over sixty hours a week while raising young children with her husband. She knew something needed to change and this retreat was her catalyst. From the moment she arrived, Tiffany completely relaxed and welcomed stillness. Her entire body came alive with excitement for her life as she began to breathe deeply again. In the stillness, Tiffany connected to a part of herself that she hadn't listened to in a long time —the part that she shoved down and out of her way so she could get her work done in an amazing business she had created. Her head had begun spinning months earlier when her dream business began to grow rapidly. Although thrilled, her family and her own sense of self were suffering. She felt like she was riding on a runaway train.

In the stillness at the VIP retreat, Tiffany remembered why she had created her business in the first place: to fit into her life, not take it over. She reorganized her priorities, putting self-care first and her family second. She committed to a food detox to help her feel her best. Tiffany restructured her life to be filled with love, fun, and a balanced amount of work, all while embracing stillness.

Samantha took a different approach to her stillness. She gradually moved away from the busyness of her out-of-control life, dipping her toes in the Being Still camp much slower than Tiffany, which was perfect for her. When Samantha got still and quiet she recognized that she was ENOUGH, and felt excited to step into her soul's purpose. She began saying no to Mr. Wrong to allow Mr. Right to enter through the front door, in his perfect timing.

It took her over a year to weed out negative friends and work situations in her life. This also included a move to an entirely new state. As she continued practicing stillness, Samantha's fears surrounding money began to surface. She didn't run from them this time. She welcomed them, recognized them, stayed aware of the fears, and let them come up — one by one. Samantha knew feeling and naming her fear would allow it to dissipate. She continues today to work with these difficult issues in the stillness, as layer upon layer are peeled away.

Jennifer is only beginning to peel away the layers of anger and resentment as she becomes STILL. It seems these strong feelings arise as quickly as the Titanic sank. After years of stuffing her feelings down with food, activities, and drama, Jennifer is now mature and feels safe being STILL to embrace these difficult feelings. Like Samantha, in the stillness, she is learning to allow the feelings to come up and dissipate, layer after layer.

When Amber left her fast-paced, big city life for her STILLNESS weekend VIP retreat with me, she experienced a transformation like no other. She was able to let go of her need to lead and control the things she couldn't change. In the stillness, Amber felt safe to allow herself to feel the emotions that came up for her. She cleared some old, deep wounds that had held her back. And, like the other participants experienced, when those feelings moved on through, what was left behind was an extraordinary gift of presence, clear thinking, and excitement to serve her soul's purpose.

Now, it's your turn. Find a comfy spot to relax. *Be Still*. Next time you sink into your *white space* time, ask yourself these questions:

- What can you give up Doing so you can BE?

- What are you hoping for? For yourself? For your business/ work? Your family?

- Can you let go of YOUR timing for the PERFECT time?

- What are you feeling in this moment? Can you name it?

- What are you looking at?

- Can you feel your God spark inside of you?

After you welcome stillness into your life, you too will begin to gradually experience moments of bliss, overcome with thankfulness, appreciation and love. You may also be more present in your life, know you are ENOUGH, and hear God clearer.

I'm finishing this chapter after learning that I have Hashimoto's disease, which is when my own immune system attacks my thyroid, wreaking havoc on many body systems. I wonder if the outcome would have been different if I hadn't pushed myself for so many years. Regardless, I'm welcoming it as a wake-up call to take even better care of myself. I'm prepared to embrace this new normal and honor myself in a more deliberate way. Now, the quality of my life depends on it.

To *Be Still* is only the beginning of this adventure of setting your spark of hope on fire. In the next chapter we will learn how to put to rest the mind chatter that holds us back.

Now it's your turn

Be Still

As you work your way through *More Than Enough*, you might want to have a notebook or journal to capture your thoughts as you reflect and implement, changing your life from the inside.

- Select a place where you can sit in comfort and silence. It can be your favorite cozy chair, or on a Zafu meditation pillow.

- Notice thoughts that stream in and out of your consciousness.

- Ponder the following questions:

- What can you eliminate from your "To Do" list so you can simply BE?

- What are your hopes for yourself, your family, your business/work?

- What would it feel like to give up your perspective of "your timing" for the "perfect time?"

- What feelings are bubbling up for you? Name them.

- What do you see? Describe it.

- As you sit in silence, are you able to hear the voice inside? What is God/the Universe saying to you?

- How long can you sit in silence? Try first ten minutes and increase it slowly up to 20 minutes.

- Once you've been still, write in your journal what came up for you, and how you felt (before, during, and after).

Silence the Mind Chatter

"Our thoughts are just a story our mind tells us."

– Romina Avila

Recently I saw an interview with the lead singer of the band Train, Patrick Monahan, who talked about being in therapy and how his therapist pointed out that in our human psyche we always have two voices we can choose to listen to. One he referred to as the angel. From that one therapy session, he wrote the moving song, Calling All Angels.

This song reminds me as well to call on my angels. In the past, I didn't even think of asking God and his angels for help. Now, it's a part of my every day. They are with me every step. Sometimes, they help me get out of bed when I haven't slept particularly well. They guide me to the places I need to go, and people I need to talk to. I ask for their support and assistance in healing, send them ahead of me to places I'm going, and call them in to carry myself and loved ones to safety when traveling. When I remember to ask for help, my Angels are ALWAYS there. They especially help me to decipher the annoying inner critic.

I want to resolve for you once and for all that you do not have to believe every single thought in your head. Our minds are constantly chatting. Some call it mind chatter. Others, monkey mind. Others may even call it the devil! Regardless, this nonstop babble going on in our minds is always going to be there. I want you to know that you do not have to believe it. You get to choose what you *listen* to!

The problem with believing the non-stop mind chatter is it can take us down faster than a punch in the stomach. We listen to this mind chatter over and over tell us: you are stupid, you are ugly, you will never amount to anything, you will never be paid a fair wage, you don't deserve more, you are not enough, you are pathetic. You can't write a book. Who do you think you are? No one wants to hear what you have to say! You begin to believe it. It's all you know. Soon, your self-esteem and self-worth are so far in the dumps you can hardly see over the mound of lies.

Mind chatter can be relentless and just about drive you nuts until you're able to recognize it for what it is... just chatter. (I love the definition of chatter: purposeless or foolish talk.) That's exactly what goes on in most of our heads daily. Foolish talk. No purpose to it.

At an early age, I would hear over and over from influential adults and other children alike you're fat, you're ugly, you're stupid, and you're worthless. Over time, they didn't even have to say it; I would repeat it in my head myself. That's all I heard. All I knew.

While in high school, once a teacher threw chalk at me for answering a question incorrectly, yelling I was stupid in the front of the class. Like many high-schoolers, my self-esteem was already fragile, let alone to be verbally beaten up in front of my peers.

The teacher may have intended to be funny, but to me, t̓
no one laughing, especially me. The most frustrating pa̲.
experience was my guidance counselor refused even to acknowledge that the teacher's actions were wrong, reinforcing to me that
I was the issue. (This is such a wakeup call to those of us who do
teach about the impact of our words and actions decades later.)

When I began to Be Still, my mind chatter increased even more.
But this time, in my silence I could *hear* it, be aware of it, and
start questioning it myself. That's another benefit of *Being Still*
– you are slowed down so you can be aware of what is really happening in your world. You begin to notice. Inevitably, the chatter
volume will increase for you as well. That's okay. Welcome it. Let
it happen.

Numerous studies have proven for every thought we think there
is a chemical reaction that sends messages throughout our body.
I knew if I began sending positive messages to my body, it would
eventually reflect that cheerful image. For example, often dread
would come over me regarding an upcoming event and I began
to feel listless, tired, angry, and even frustrated, thinking about
what may or may not happen.

As I began noticing the negative thoughts, I could reframe them
to envision my ideal outcome. I would focus on the best case sce-
nario, not the worst. It wasn't long before my mood improved with
a brighter outlook. With each reframe of the negative thoughts,
my energy also seemed to magically increase.

As you hear the mind chatter speaking foolish talk, acknowledge
it. Experts on this topic differ on their opinions. Some say to ignore it and let it pass. Others encourage you to recognize it for
what it is – foolish talk – and to tell yourself the opposite. For

example, if your mind chatter repeatedly tells you, "You are fat. I can't believe you're even thinking of eating today," in your stillness, you become aware of the thought running in your mind and turn it around and say back to yourself, "I am beautifully and wonderfully made. I am healthy, healed, and whole. Everything I eat benefits me." Use the method that works best for you.

For whatever reason, I didn't know that the talk inside my head wasn't necessarily true or that I could decide whether to believe it. Once I realized I could control my thoughts, my life changed! I no longer believed everything my head screamed at me! I could sit back and let it chatter all it wanted while I chose what was true and what wasn't.

Once I became aware of this 24/7 recording going on in the background of my mind, my life gradually opened to new possibilities. I began to see clearly how my thoughts (conscious or not) were creating my future. I recognized ahead of time when I was headed down a downhill and chose to change the recording playing. Eventually, the spark inside me began to light up with excitement for life. My self-esteem increased. Depression lifted. Confidence soared. I began to believe in myself and feel a purpose for living. I came alive day-by-day as I changed the recording of the mind chatter.

A Type-A super smart client, Michael, recently came to me for help with a recurring mind chatter loop. His chatter sent him on a slide toward hopelessness. The same messages replayed over and over in his mind. Experiencing frustration and aggravation, he couldn't break the circular thinking. When we talked, he acknowledged that he was well aware of the mind chatter, but didn't know how to stop the maddening thoughts. Michael was partially trying the second method of being aware of the mind chatter but he wasn't able to turn the thoughts into something positive yet. He was trying to make sense of the foolish talk when there was no sense to be made! So, we tried a different approach. I encouraged him to ignore it instead! Sometimes when one method doesn't work, you try the other one. And, this was the best solution for Michael.

When the thoughts entered his mind, he was aware but allowed them to pass through and got busy doing something he enjoyed. Next time I talked to him, he was relaxed, energized, and thrilled that he could enjoy his life again without the same maddening, debilitating thoughts replaying in his mind.

My client Jennifer, previously mentioned in the Be Still chapter, also struggles with a mind that doesn't stop chattering, even to the point of not sleeping at night. Sometimes, she pushes herself to stay super busy so she doesn't have to slow down and hear her chatter.

Instead of ignoring the thoughts, like Michael, Jennifer embraced reframing her thoughts. In the stillness, she heard the thoughts that came up. Mostly, her thoughts were of fear and frustration, reminding her of all the things she should be doing differently or better at work and at home. She allowed these thoughts to run her life. They began to take over her life, even causing illness in her body, before she came to me for assistance. I explained how for every thought we think there is a chemical reaction that is sent out into our body. No wonder her body was reacting to these negative thoughts!

As Jennifer acknowledged and reframed the recordings into a positive light, her fear subsided, confidence soared, and she began feeling peace over her body. I suspect more positive talk sent out happy chemicals to her body to help it calm down and heal.

Nowadays, I have quite a different relationship with my mind chatter. (Oh, it's always there!) I normally acknowledge it, decide whether it's truth and Christ-like (or from the angels, like Patrick Monahan says) and then choose to let it pass through or accept it. When you choose not to believe all that the foolish chatter is telling you, you can tell it the truth and have an entirely different outlook on life. In the next chapter, we will tap into what comes after you get still and *Silence the Mind Chatter*, and that is *Mindfulness and Meditation*.

I encourage you to listen to the voices in your own head. I suspect that if you're suffering from low self-worth, you've been listening to a voice that tells you such. Now, it's time to relax and let that negative mind chatter pass right on through or reframe the message. And, *Calling All Angels* isn't a bad idea either!

Now it's your turn

Silence The Mind Chatter

As you work your way through *More Than Enough*, you might want to have a notebook or journal to capture your thoughts as you reflect and implement, changing your life from the inside.

- Select a place where you can sit in comfort and silence. It can be your favorite cozy chair, on a Zafu meditation pillow, or anywhere you can spend time in stillness and quiet.

- Notice thoughts that stream in and out of your consciousness.

- What chatter occurs as you sit in still? Can you simply notice these thoughts and allow them to pass by like bubbles?

- Ponder the following questions:

  - What can you eliminate from your "To Do" list so you can simply BE?

  - What are your hopes for yourself, your family, your business/work?

  - What would it feel like to give up your perspective of "your timing" for the "perfect time?"

  - What feelings are bubbling up for you? Name them.

  - What do you see? Describe it.

- As you sit in silence, are you able to hear the voice inside? What is God/the Universe saying to you?

- How long can you sit in silence? Try first ten minutes and increase it slowly up to 20 minutes.

Once you've been still, write in your journal what came up for you, and how you felt (before, during, and after). See if you are able to reframe thoughts which no longer serve you into phrases or mantras which support you where you are now.

Mindfulness and Meditation

"Be happy in the moment, That's enough.
Each moment is all we need, not more."

– Mother Teresa

In *The Mindful Way through Depression*, Mark Williams wrote:

> *Start living right here, in each present moment. When*
> *we stop dwelling on the past or worrying about the fu-*
> *ture, we're open to rich sources of information we've been*
> *missing out on—information that can keep us out of the*
> *downward spiral and poised for a richer life.*

Everywhere I go people want to push on me their way of being mindful and meditating. There are even proper ways to breathe now. I can never seem to do anything right by the experts' standards. Well-meaning teachers insist their way is the only way and I'm doing it all wrong. Nothing is more frustrating to me!

Let me begin by saying I'm not an expert on this topic. However, I know what has worked for me, and what is right for me and my life.

For our purposes, the "right way" is whatever way feels right to you! Just as there are many roads leading to the same destination, it is the same for mindfulness and meditation.

There are hundreds, if not thousands, of books and articles written on mindfulness, meditation, and breathing. I'm not even sure that I can do it justice condensing it into one small chapter. What I invite you to do, though, is start. Begin a practice of learning about these subjects and becoming aware of the huge impact and benefit they can have on your life. Learn the basics. Don't shy away from meditating thinking it's something woo-woo.

For decades, I was told by the church not to meditate or do yoga because those were against God. That's very odd, because when I'm practicing meditation, I feel closer to God than EVER. Meditating allows me to connect to God on a level that can only be done one- on-one. For me, prayer is when I'm doing all the talking to God. In meditation, I finally get quiet enough to HEAR. I listen to what God is saying to me!

As I embraced *Mindfulness and Meditation*, I felt an all-around peace. My thoughts were clearer; my energy was focused. Life had an easier ebb and flow. Messages were crystal clear. I began to sense, see and hear angels. The more I surrendered my agenda, my expectations, and my ego, God was able to speak to me in a powerful way.

I don't know what to call or label it. In the church and in healing circles, it's often called speaking in tongues or Angel Speak. All I know is that this beautiful language pouring from me could move mountains. People are healed. They have said they feel lighter, and often have a skip in their step. Others feel as though they've just had a chiropractic adjustment and rest is usually in order while they assimilate whatever healing God orchestrated. What it does for others, it does for me as well. All because I began to meditate and to be open to God's possibilities for my life.

My family and friends could tell something was different, but couldn't quite put their fingers on it. Although some may argue this point, I even became much more patient! I started enjoying the little things in life. Even doing the dishes became an enjoyable activity!

Practicing *Mindfulness and Meditation* will allow you to look at your life from a new perspective. From the inside out, which may be easier on some days than others, but is always rewarding. It starts with *Being Still*, quieting the mind chatter and next, digging deeper.

Embarking on this sort of practice might seem daunting. Let me take the scariness out of it for you by providing a simple guide to get started. Often the words, *Mindfulness and Meditation*, are used interchangeably. Part of the confusion stems from the fact that they both have numerous meanings. However, they are quite different. For our purposes, I'll share an easy way to differentiate the two.

– Mindfulness –

Mindfulness means being aware or focusing on something intently; being in the present moment. During meditation, you are being mindful. But you can also be mindful throughout your day during various activities, such as: as you drive,e at, play with your kids or talk on the phone with a friend. Mindfulness has been embraced by millions of people. You find it in the boardroom (Google), the classroom (various school districts), and even within our government.

Here are some top ways to be mindful throughout your day:

- Eat slowly and with focus. Enjoy each bite along with your company and the atmosphere you are experiencing.

- Focus on the person who is in front of you as you are talking to them.

- Be 100% present no matter what you are doing — writing an email, texting, driving, working out, walking on the beach, eating, doing the dishes, talking to your children, playing. Whatever you do — do it with all of you!

According to *Doing and Being: Mindfulness, Health, and Quiet Ego Characteristics among Buddhist Practitioners*, the 2011 research article that published the survey results in the Journal of Happiness Studies [12(4): 575-589], there were five key ways that mindfulness training increased physical and mental health.

1. It strengthened the immune system and physiological responses to stress and negative emotions.

2. It improved social relationships with family and strangers.

3. It reduced stress, depression, and anxiety while it increased well-being and happiness.

4. It increased openness to experience, conscientiousness, and agreeableness plus reduced negative associations with neuroticism.

5. It led to greater psychological mindfulness, which included an awareness that is clear, non-conceptual, and flexible; a practical stance toward reality; and present attention to the individual's consciousness and awareness.

– Meditation –

The official definition of Meditation is to engage in contemplation or reflection, usually with a focused mental intent or a single point of reference. According to *Psychology Today*:

> *It can involve focusing on the breath, on bodily sensations, or on a word or phrase known as a mantra. In other words, meditation means turning your attention away from distracting thoughts and focusing on the present moment.*

I begin and end each day with prayer and meditation. When I first began meditating, I used a guided meditation which helped me relax while staying focused. As my skill increased in this area, I was able to take a few deep breathes before dropping into the space of openness in almost an instant. When I'm seeking guidance on important issues in my life, meditation is always my first stop. I invite you to look within your own heart for God's direction for your life.

Let's practice being in the present moment.

While you are Being Still, you will most likely begin to hear some mind chatter. It's nothing that you need to concern yourself with. Choose to let it pass through along with your endless to-do list. Instead, focus on the love in your heart. That is your true essence.

Don't give up. Sit and enjoy that white space in your day. At first, this time may feel awkward and non-productive. Acknowledge that's how you feel and move on.

Next, close your eyes and breathe.

Take a deep breath and feel your breath come up one side of your body. Hold for four seconds. Release slowly, feeling it go down the other side of your body. Do this three times.

Now, envision your heart by focusing your attention on your heart. Can you feel it pumping? Can you feel the love inside of it? Imagine the love growing inside of you. What does it feel like? Scan the rest of your body. What are you feeling? Are there any emotions that are coming up? If so, feel them. One-by-one. One-by-one. One-by-one. Acknowledge them. Name the feelings. Let them pass through you.

If you feel like crying, do. Let feelings flow through you. Let whatever must come up for the day, come up and out. Let it flow. Move out of your body. Feel your body becoming lighter and lighter as emotion after emotion is dealt with and moved through. Acknowledge all that needs to come up throughout the day. Thank your body for its work and the processing it does for you.

Encourage yourself for the day. What words of affirmation can you tell yourself to support you today? For example, it's going to be a great day. Or, I am healthy, healed and whole.

Set your intention for the day. What do you want to accomplish? What do you want to do today that will make it a GREAT day? Do you need to call anyone? How can you show up for your life today? Set that intention.

While you're still indoors, imagine yourself standing on the green grass, and feel the grass beneath your bare feet. Luxuriate in it for about four seconds and then open your eyes. What you have experienced is meditation. Meditation is not some rah-rah woo-

woo new age thing. It is real. Try it, and then tell me you didn't feel better!

I encourage all my clients to take time each day to meditate. It's too important to miss.

The benefits of *Mindfulness and Meditation* are mind-blowing. Studies have shown in meditation, EVERY cell in the body fills with more energy which results in joy, peace, and enthusiasm.

Specifically, here are a few other benefits:

- Reduces stress/Decreases anxiety.
- Adds clarity and peace of mind.
- Lowers high blood pressure.
- Decreases tension in the body.
- Increases serotonin production.
- Improves the immune system.
- Increases the energy level.
- Improves concentration.
- Encourages healthy lifestyle.
- Problems shrink.
- Brings to mind solutions.

The great news about meditation is that the results are cumulative. As you embrace the practice, the benefits accumulate.

After some initial hesitation, Tiffany relaxed while listening to a guided meditation during a one-on-one session with me. There were tears, laughs, even surprise as she melted into the words and images that God showed her. As she sprung up from this new experience, she smiled with a sense of awe new to her. In the days following, Tiffany still vividly remembered the clear messages she received during meditation and the calmness that followed. Noticing enormous benefits, she makes time almost daily now for a shorter meditation.

Jennifer was also new to meditation but eager to learn. She began with small amounts of time – five to ten minutes here and there. Usually, she used a guided meditation downloaded from the internet. Other times, she played soft music while she quieted her mind. After a few weeks, Jennifer began to notice subtle changes in how she reacted to events in her life. She was more patient with her husband and children. She didn't seem as angry at the little mishaps during the day. Overall, Jennifer felt happier and more at peace, which she attributed to the cumulative effects of meditation.

Evan, seasoned meditator, had never used it for anything other than his personal life. As Evan and I worked together, we focused on a guided meditation to take his business to the next level. This shift resulted in a remarkable experience, which he still uses even months later. He saw more clearly the health of his business and gleaned information that helped him restructure his business to be more profitable, while helping his clients at an even deeper level.

Like Jennifer, Tiffany, and Evan, I can't imagine my life without meditation. My life has transformed partly due to this one practice alone. It quickly centers me and provides a reset anytime, anywhere. This, too, could be your go-to for reducing the stress in your daily life.

Where meditating requires quiet, eyes-closed, inner focus, going outside in nature asks us to open our eyes to soak in the beauty surrounding us. In the next chapter, we will look more closely at the benefits of spending time outdoors.

I can't promise that when you begin to meditate you'll see angels or speak unknown healing words; that's between you and God. At first, you may see progress in terms of physical relaxation and emotional calmness. Later, you may notice other, subtler changes. Some of the most important benefits of meditation make themselves known over time and are not dramatic or easily observed. Persist in your practice and you will find that meditation frees you from the worries that gnaw at you. By opening up space inside, you are free to experience the joy of being fully present, here and now.

Now it's your turn

Mindfulness and Meditation

Here are a few top ways to practice mindfulness throughout your day. Choose the one(s) which feel

- Chew your food slowly and with focus. Savor the flavors and textures. Soak in the atmosphere in which you enjoy your meals.

- Focus on the person with whom you are in a conversation. Look into their eyes and listen to each word without reacting or forming a response.

- Choose one activity to do and focus on it completely.

- Turn off electronic devices during meals, when you're driving, and when you're working.

- Choose specific times to open and respond to emails.

Here are a few tips to get you started on your own meditation journey.

- Schedule your meditation time and keep your commitment to it.

- Tell your family, friends, and co-workers not to disturb you during your meditation time.

- Select a quiet room in your home and/or office to meditate.

- Choose on what you'll sit to meditate. For example, you can sit on a sofa, a Zafu meditation pillow, or your bed.

- Set up your space to encourage quiet contemplation.

- Set a timer for your mediation (I like the chime sound effect to ring at the end of my meditation). Begin with two or three minutes and work your way up to 20.

- Start by focusing on your breath, taking deep inhalations into your belly and slowly exhaling through your nose. Some people find counting to four helpful: four as you breath in, hold for four, exhale for four, and leave space for four before beginning the cycle again.

- Decide if you want to meditate on your own or if a guided meditation might serve you.

- Select a mantra or focus phrase.

- Let thoughts float in and out of your mind without judging them or you. Come back to your mantra.

- Let go of expectations.

Here are a few meditation apps you might consider trying:

- Buddify

- Calm

- Headspace

- Omvana

- Take a Break

- Simply Being

The Healing Effects of Nature

"Nature itself is the best medicine."

– Hippocrates

Have you ever stood at the ocean's edge? Relished the sound and feel of the crashing waves? Or reveled in the beautiful mountains of Sedona? Maybe hiking is your thing. How do you feel when you are in the midst of nature's beauty? Balanced? Centered? Relaxed?

As I write this chapter, I'm enjoying the view of a gorgeous Japanese garden at the Four Season's Westlake Village, California. As I walked the gardens, I came alive. The worries of the day melted away, and I soaked up the incredible beauty.

Often, on a daily basis, we're handling life as if it comes at us, fast and furious. We spend our days putting out fires, which causes other emotional, physical, and psychological issues.

We can't sleep. We clench our teeth. We forgot to breathe. We forget who we are.

The stress from the pressure cooker of life increases in the body until we become anxious, angry, and sink into depression. All this from our everyday life of living!

The past decade had been traumatic in my personal life. I experienced four of the top five stressors: family member deaths, divorce, moving, and major illness. As if those weren't enough, I also had computers stolen, became an empty nester, and indured a flood. No wonder I felt as though my life were topsy turvy!

Nature was an integral part of healing me through this difficult period.

As stress mounted in my life, I knew it was time for me to take a different route. I was at a point in my life where my health challenges and past traumas affected my daily quality of living. The approaching winter months in the Midwest concerned me. Indiana's cloudy winter days combined with cold temperatures and snow often led to my depression. Thus, I decided to become a snowbird and flew south to the ocean!

Typically, a snowbird is a retiree who chooses to avoid the snow or cold by living in a warmer climate for a few months out of each year. I've always been drawn to various beaches for short vacations, so this was an easy decision for me, as I knew it would provide a natural location that would support my healing. Just think: two solid months of rest, relaxation, and just being.

The daily walks on the beach, viewing sunsets over the ocean and relaxing on the Island became an integral part of the routine supporting my body as it healed. Walking on the sand, I envisioned past traumas washing out into the ocean depths, never to be seen again. Each forward step into the life I wanted to live allowed me to let go of something else. Emotions were released from the deepest of cells in my body. Some days I would walk with tears of sorrow. Other days, tears of joy.

Regardless of the reason, the ocean and sunsets provided a background of beauty and support that assisted me in a myriad of ways.

Playing in nature helped me to:

- Mend my broken heart.
- Release self-limiting beliefs that were holding me back.
- Release old patterns and open to unlimited possibilities.
- Reconnect to my soul's desire to enjoy the beauty of life.
- Reconnect with my own spark of hope.
- Renew my commitment to my self-care and self-worth.
- Renew my spiritual connection.
- Renew my commitment to pursuing my greatest dreams.

All that because I chose to walk along the ocean's edge and view the sunsets at any opportunity! Author Wallace J. Nichols wrote about the fascinating connection between nature and healing in *Blue Mind: The Surprising Science That Shows How Being Near, In, On, or Under Water Can Make You Happier, Healthier, More Connected, and Better at What You Do*. He said, "Like a child depends upon its mother, humans have always depended upon nature for our survival. And just as we intuitively love our mothers, we are linked to nature physically, cognitive and emotionally."

In the early 80s, a researcher in Paoli, Pennsylvania collected information about patients who had undergone gallbladder surgery over a nine-year period. The research investigated the difference in patients' recoveries based on the orientation of the patients' hospital beds. Some patients' beds faced a brick wall and others faced a stand of trees. Apart from their differing views, the rooms were identical. The results may not surprise you. On average, those who faced the brick wall needed an extra day to recover before returning home. They were far more depressed and experienced more pain. Interestingly, only a few of the patients who looked onto the trees required more than a single dose of strong painkillers during the middle part of their stay compared to those facing the wall, who required two or even three doses.

Studies repeatedly have shown that hanging out in nature can lower blood pressure, reduce anxiety, relieve stress, sharpen mental states. It can even help those suffering from ADHD disorders, depression, addictions, insomnia, stress, and more. Nature tends to bring out the best in each of us. It soothes, heals, restores, and connects us.

My older brother also had an amazing experience with nature. Years ago, he had a landscape business and planted hundreds of trees in his backyard. He told me that watching them grow was his church.

Recently, I spent several days hiking beautiful Mount Shasta in Northern California. This trip was a last minute add-on to a week of non-stop meetings. The quietness of the forest almost immediately reset my body and mind. Hiking seems to be very healing for me. The rhythm of putting each foot in front of the other allowed my mind to wander. I did a walking meditation to keep silent and Be Still. I wanted to be present. To soak in every noise, every tree rustle. To hear every footfall and each bird chirping. Before long I had forgotten all about the Los Angeles traffic!

As I hiked uphill, dodging boulders in the pathway, I noticed how different emotions surfaced. Sometimes my thoughts made me laugh but mostly I cried! As I let the emotions pass through without trying to figure them out or judge them, I felt stronger. Even my hiking pattern changed. Instead of walking around boulders in my way, I stepped ON THEM for leverage to go higher, further, faster! What a lesson from nature: step on the boulders in our life! Those "boulders" that are seemingly in our way may be there to launch us even further at a faster rate. Instead of trying to side-step the obstacle, embrace it, put your foot on top, and let it give you a stronger leverage to propel you into your future.

For whatever reason, hiking and being out in nature seemed to escalate the kind of healing achieved by processing emotions. By the time I left Mount Shasta, I felt transformed — centered, grounded, relaxed, and quiet. What better place to release past hurts and sadness than surrounded by God's beauty?

Samantha had a demanding corporate job with an overflowing inbox where she stared at a computer screen all day. Even though lunch was brought in daily for staff members, Samantha usually packed her lunch so she could sit outside and enjoy it in the quiet. Usually, right after she ate, she took a short walk around the block before returning to her desk, filled inbox, and computer screen. Samantha says that since she began her practice, her mental clarity and focus are stronger than ever, especially in the afternoon when most people's energy drops.

If you're a person who doesn't normally spend time outdoors, I challenge you to start with a fifteen minute walk outside every evening. Notice how you feel before and afterward. Do you feel more centered? Balanced? Energized? Focused? Just notice and follow those feelings of bliss.

In the next chapter, we're going to talk about setting up your life for success. Being in nature is an integral part of that success and can also help facilitate this difficult step in renewing your commitment to yourself.

There are hundreds of other studies outlining the benefits of spending time outdoors. What is important to note from these studies is the overall consensus is... spend time outdoors, with others, every day. This will provide the well-needed restorative experience your body craves to be in balance. And, isn't that what a family beach vacation does? Soak up the grass, flowers, sun, waves, mountains, trees, rocks, streams...let them balance you and reconnect with the true you, which is complete self-love!

Now It's Your Turn

The Healing Effects of Nature

- How much time do you spend outdoors? Can you increase it by 15-minutes a day?

- Do you prefer the beach to the mountains or vice versa? Schedule time to visit your favorite.

- Do you prefer walking through your neighborhood or hiking a wooded trail?

- Make a list of potential activities you can do outdoors, even those you haven't yet tried but are willing to.

- Schedule one new activity a month, outside your regular daily outdoor time. Here are a few ideas to get you started:

  - A visit to a botanical garden

  - Gardening

  - Watching the sunset or sunrise

  - Walking/hiking

  - Kayaking

  - Skipping stones at a lake or bay

  - Swimming

  - Golfing (real or miniature)

  - Biking

  - Visit a zoo or conservatory

- Jot down in your journal how you're feeling before your nature-time and then notice the difference, if any, afterward. Jot down your observations.

- Create a playlist of songs to enjoy while you're outdoors. Consider NOT making a playlist and noticing the sounds of nature.

- Spend time with a loved one on an evening walk.

Sleep, Schedules and Surroundings

"You should deeply care about what you think, what you want, what you need, and what makes you feel happy. Just as important, you should have plans and routines in place that allow you to do all these things and care for yourself in general."

– Brendon Burchard

Success reminds me of watching my boys in the Avon (High School) Marching Black & Gold Band, aka AMB&G. They would work for hours and hours on the same thirty seconds of the show. Over and over again so it would be perfect. Their bodies would remember what to do even when they were exhausted. They could do it in their sleep.

During the same hours, the kids were on the field, parents, and other employees were stocking Gatorade and energy bars for competitions, building and sewing props, writing music, cleaning and fixing instruments, polishing shoes, matching socks, ironing uniforms, preparing first aid kits, and more. All the parts work together – the staff (paid and volunteer), students, and parents blend their time and talents into a six-month season and hundreds of hours on the field. Even when the student was at home, rest, and nutrition were still a high priority to keep their bodies functioning at a high level. When it was show time, 300 students of the AMB&G took the field doing their thing like a well-oiled machine. The three- time Grand National Champions and 13-time Indiana State Winning trophies tell the story of success.

What would happen if the AMB&G hadn't honed their program? For starters, they wouldn't have won all the awards and accolades that they have. Their performances would also be complete chaos. Students would run into each other on the field. Who knows what might happen off the field with the parents and staff! Instruments might be broken; students would be hungry, thirsty, and tired; uniforms would be wrinkled and ripped. These are just a few issues lack of organization and structure can cause.

In our lives, incomplete structures create chaos, as well. We might wing it when it comes to our daily responsibilities. Dishes might not washed and dried. But then again, maybe we wouldn't even have groceries to cook and would need to eat most of our meals out. Forget beds ever being made or home projects ever being completed. Eating healthy and working out would be something that would never enter your mind because there wouldn't be *time* for such splurges. You might sleep in because you stayed up late watching TV; you had no schedule the next day, and you always felt like you couldn't get everything on your "To do" list done.

Your surroundings would be filled with clutter, unpacked boxes, memories of unmet dreams, and stuff that no longer represented you. This *stuff* held you back from moving forward in your life without you even knowing it.

I often wondered what it would take to live life like a well-oiled machine—smooth, a daily flow, seldom rushed, enjoyed, not endured, full of beauty, love, and adventure. For me, I saw that it would take a life embedded with structures in the background that kept me going even when I didn't *feel* like it.

Structures provide an arrangement for the parts of our lives that we need to set us up for success on a daily basis. Being the creative, multi-faceted, spiritual woman that I am who wants to remain flexible without expectation or judgment, so I resist structure sometimes. (Okay, most of the time!) It's not that I don't desire structure. I do. I love to be organized and have systems in place, but I resist structuring my day because I want to be open in the moment to where or what God is leading me. I already have enough material to write a whole different book on being led by God in the moment, but for now, suffice it to say, every day is an adventure!

These days, to run a successful business and write powerful books that will help people know they are enough, I've merged my openness to God creating a Spirit-led schedule which integrates my daily responsibilities. Yearly goals down to daily schedules are prayed over and tweaked as I'm led.

This partnership has set my life and business up for success while still allowing me to be open to God's flow. Three of the main areas that helped me to oil my machine called *life* were sleep, schedules, and surroundings.

– Sleep –

After several bouts of mononucleosis, adrenal exhaustion, and thyroid disease, I have learned the importance of sleep. I'm a slow learner! When my body doesn't get the proper amount of sleep, you can bet that nothing else in my body or day is going to work properly either! And, for you, I suspect it's the same. Having a great day on Tuesday starts Monday night, by getting to bed at an hour that sets you up for success.

Although during the last decade I struggled to sleep at night, a few months ago I went through a time I slept ten hours a night plus napped! When I was awake, I would go for a short walk and worked as best I could. I honored this unusual schedule my body craved, while, of course, hoping it wouldn't last too long! I began to feel guilty. Why? Because that's what we are conditioned to feel if we're not performing at optimum levels on a regular basis.

I say that's all fine and good, but when our bodies are suffering through our pushing, we're not doing anyone any favors. We get run down. Exhausted. Cranky! That long period of rest for me cameafter months of a very stressful time in my life. My body was demanding a BREAK!

Our bodies are these beautiful masterpieces, an intricate tapestry, if you will, that need to be loved and treated with respect. Especially as we age. When we're younger, we can get away with less sleep, even more junk food. But as we get older, we're not quite as resilient. It's important to connect to your body on a daily, maybe hourly, basis. Listen to what it's trying to tell you. Don't ignore the signs before it's screaming at you that something more serious is wrong.

Daily life can be stressful. The best thing we can do is to honor our bodies on a regular basis as we ride the waves of life. That's true self-love.

I remind you today to honor your body. Become aware of its need to REST and offer it what it is asking. You'll be amazed at the outcome. Whether your body is calling for a good night's sleep or a Rip Van Winkle kind of sleep, you'll be amazed at the outcome. When your body is done oversleeping, you'll naturally come back into balance.

My client, Sally, struggled to get to sleep and stay asleep at night. She was of menopause-age flooded with fluctuating hormones that caused a massive disruption in her sleep cycle. As the disruption lingered, she began to experience issues during the day. She felt listless when she should have been wide awake. She depended on caffeine to help her keep up with her busy schedule. The caffeine only made her feel defeated and frustrated with herself. I encouraged her to get a full panel of hormone tests and begin working with a physician to correct any hormone imbalance as well as adding in a natural sleep supplement.

A few weeks later, Sally was smiling from ear to ear because she was finally sleeping soundly and deeply, while her body was adjusting to the naturally balanced hormones.

– Schedules –

Aristotle wrote, "We are what we repeatedly do." As mentioned earlier, I knew intuitively that schedules were important, but I resisted following one! I created schedules, but not follow them, and then berated myself for not following the schedule that I set!

Jana Kingsford said, "Balance is not something you find, it's something you create." To balance means, something is used to produce equilibrium. In our daily lives, there are more than two things we need to do daily to balance the scale. We juggle hundreds of activities each month that need to weigh evenly on our scale of daily activities. Instead of thinking that you need to balance your life, envision each activity you partake in as a spoke on a wheel, a piece of your life that needs oil to run smoothly.

In our case of daily responsibilities and living life with the goal of ease and flow, to balance our lives, in my opinion, means to blend all activities that we need to live a full life. Scheduling sleep, work, play, relationship connections, healthy meals, and workouts every day sets you up to skyrocket your self-worth and self-love. You're no good to anyone if all you do is work constantly. Life is about living, loving, and relationships.

For you, it might mean only working four hours a day. Who says we all have to work forty hours a week? And, why can't that work be done while you're overlooking a beautiful beach or mountain top? Design your life and business around what YOU LOVE. This is self- love, which means taking care of yourself FIRST and then adding other important routines into your schedule. Most people make the mistake of creating their lives the other way around.

I ask clients what their morning and evening routines look like. Their responses are to gaze at me with wide eyes because they have no routine! I totally get it. I didn't have any problem showing up for other people but I neglected myself. When I began a morning routine it became a sacred time where I showed up for ME. And, what I learned was following an established routine not only set me up for a successful day, it fueled an increase to my self-esteem and was an act of self- love. Again, each conscious act contributed to my life becoming a well-oiled machine.

Darren Hardy talks about the power of routines in his book, *The Compound Effect*. He says:

A routine is something you do every day without fail, so that eventually, like brushing your teeth or putting on your seatbelt, you do it without conscious thought... To establish profitable and effective routines, you must first decide what behaviors and habits you want to implement.

Think about what YOU need to fuel yourself for the day. For me it was quiet time, coffee, prayer, meditation, and a workout. Write down your non-negotiables in your calendar and commit this time to yourself. This is a beautiful act of self-love!

My client Michael, whom I mentioned earlier in the book, schedules his day from sun up till sun down with daily responsibilities and activities and builds in little creative time. After becoming ill, he realized he was not living his purpose. Michael came to me unsure how to infuse creative time relating to his passion into a solid schedule. We discussed utilizing a few hours of focused time each day where Facebook, email, and texting were shut off so he could focus strictly on his creative project. After only a week of this new schedule, Michael was astonished by how much he had accomplished by shutting down the unnecessary for the important creative work he needed to do.

On a daily basis, I'm always asking God and his angels for assistance to accomplish what I need to and let the rest go. When I do ask, my day falls into place, maybe not how I would have planned it, but perfect nonetheless. Regardless of the system you use—digital, paper, or a combo—spend some time in prayer asking God for guidance. We all have unique needs and purposes, and we process information differently. No one schedule is perfect for everyone. Let your schedule be set with guidance from the Heavens to propel you to be your best YOU. It's amazing how the important items get done seamlessly while the unimportant fall away. There is even time left over for fun!

– Surroundings –

In *The Compound Effect*, Darren Hardy says, "Everyone is affected by three kinds of influences: input (what you feed your mind), associations (the people with whom you spend time with), and environment (your surroundings)."

Because I'm super sensitive and empathetic, I tend to be a bit picky about my environment, the food I eat, the people I'm around, and what I listen to (or don't). I like a calm mindset, things clean and in order, the TV off (generally).

I know what feeds my soul and I try every day to do as many of those things as possible that help me feel better. Last winter I moved south just to stay warm. I KNEW my environment needed to change, even if for a short time.

Recently I downsized, or rather right-sized, to a house almost half the size what I lived in for twenty-five years. I was in the process of finishing this book, but surrounded by a hundred full boxes and many unfinished projects in the new house. Talk about feeling overwhelmed! Being the determined, resourceful woman that I am, I called for HELP! An angel arrived at my door by the name of Diane Halfman (DianeHalfman.com). She helped me unpack, scale down, clear out over forty years of clutter, and put solid structures in place to make this well-oiled machine run pristinely.

I've always been an organized person,(love my label maker!), but Diane took organizing to a level that amazed me! Being organized means having a formal structure, especially to coordinate or carry out widespread activities. This was exactly what I needed her for... to set up my physical space so it would support me to carry out the future activities of my business and life. It was emotional, exhausting, and exhilarating – all at the same time!

In addition to being an expert at evaluating her client's personal environments, Diane Halfman was also an Ultimate Game of Life Coach (TheUltimateGameOfLife.com). She was passionate about connecting and collaborating with others to help them gain clarity on living in their ultimate personal spaces—physically, mentally and spiritually. She moved people from overwhelming circumstances. While she was making magic organizing my belongings, she talked about the Ultimate Environment.

According to the TheUltimateGameOfLife.com website:

Most people think they need more information on how-to create more wealth, create better health, and be happier. There is some truth in the idea that you need to know the proper how-to, because if you are practicing the wrong behavior daily, you are guaranteed a negative result.

The missing element for the 95% who don't succeed is a concept called The Ultimate Environments of You. There are 9 Environments that control the way you think, the way you feel, and the way you act. In order to play your biggest game you must understand the environments that are working with you and upgrade the environments that are working against you. When you feel stress, struggle, or delay in reaching your goals, you have most likely created environments that are working against you and your goals, instead of pulling you towards your goals.

Setting nine environments up for success was the key to propelling forward business and life goals. They include these areas: Self, Spiritual, Relationships, Network, Financial, Physical, Nature, Body, and You. Since my boxes were unpacked and my surroundings were organized, I was able to focus intently on this important book, without worry.

Natalie came to me frustrated because she wasn't able to make any progress in her home business. She felt her life's work was full of struggle and blockages. When we began to dismantle her belief system, it became apparent that she really wasn't stuck in her business at all but she was holding tight to the past, all the while trying to move forward. Her house had become a museum, paying homage to the days gone by. I encouraged her to go through each item in the house, especially through her memory albums. Really sitting with them, feeling whatever came up. Holding each item. She asked herself questions like, "Do I really need this? What does it represent to me? Was it important? Is it now important? Do I need it to move forward with me?" Natalie did the hard work required on her surroundings. She said it wasn't easy. As a matter of fact, although it was one of the hardest things she had ever done, it was well worth it. Clearing her surroundings of the past allowed her to live in the moment and soar into the future!

When you implement the proper Sleep, Schedules, and Surroundings for your life, you will be amazed at the results. What was chaos transformed to now be an organized, enjoyable, smooth flow. Your life will move like efficiently, and you'll be eager to embrace the present and live out your bravest dream.

After you set yourself up for success in your sleep, schedules and surroundings, you'll also feel more equipped to usher in the next chapter's mission to know deep down that you are enough exactly as you are.

Whether we know it or not, our surroundings affect us and our daily work. If you're feeling stuck or not able to move forward in an area of your life, review these environments and, specifically, your surroundings. Take the time to clear out clutter and sift through the past so you can move into your future with ease and flow. Most importantly, know what success means to you. We all have a different idea of what success looks like in our lives. Don't let someone else's viewpoint be yours! Know yourself and you will know what success means to you.

Now it's your turn

Sleep, Schedule, and Surroundings

Here's where to begin to establish your baseline:

1. Track the hours you sleep each night and then rate the quality of your sleep. Do this for at least a week. Notate in your journal how you felt upon waking each morning.

2. Track your time and where and how you spend it. Be sure to include family time, 1:1 with your partner time, friend time, outdoor time, spiritual time, meditation time, client/work time, and downtime.

3. Walk through your home, stopping in each room. Write down in your journal the immediate feeling and word that pops into your mind as you enter each one. Don't evaluate the feelings or judge the words you select.

Sleep

- Honor your body and give it the rest it needs.

- If you can, increase your sleep by 15 minutes each night until you reach the recommended eight hours.

- If you feel like a Rip van Winkle nap is in order, listen to your body.

Schedule

- Use a calendar, paper or electronic, whatever suits you best. Block chunks of time to work on specific tasks. Honor your commitments to yourself.

- Mark days and time where you'll take care of yourself. You might schedule a massage or lunch with a friend, a walk or visit to a museum. Feed your body and soul first.

- Schedule sleep, play, connection time, meditation, journaling, time to shop for healthy food, and time to work-out or get into nature.

- Look at routines: morning and evening. What are you doing when you first wake up and just before you go to bed? Are these habits serving you?

Surroundings

- Look back at your notes regarding your living space. What areas would you like to change to enhance your life?

- If you stress over having a clean house, give yourself permission to hire a cleaning service.

- Sort through things you have and keep only those items which bring you joy.

- Tidy up before going to bed.

- Remember your surroundings include all environments: self, spiritual, relationships, network, financial, physical, nature, and body.

Additional Resources:

- *Your Best Year* by Darren Hardy

- *Better than Before* by Gretchen Rubin (also, *Happier at Home*)

- *Miracle Morning* by Hal Elrod

- *Mindset* by Carol Dweck

Rock What You've Got

*"You are enough. You have nothing
to prove to anybody."*

– Maya Angelou

Dear Body:

I loathe you. I hate that you don't look the way I want you to. That you aren't a perfect size 0. I hate that I push you and push you and you fight me by gaining weight or making my hair fall out. I hate that you aren't perfect. I hate that I have to take care of you and you still don't look like I want you to. It's very frustrating. I hate that you can't or won't do all that I ask. There is so much in my life I want to do and you aren't there for me. Why won't you do what you're supposed to do? How can I love you if you're not perfect?

Sad to say, that was my journal entry only a few years ago. There was no self-love to be found in my life at that time. I had this image in my head of what a perfect body was, but that wasn't necessarily God's plan. He created each of us perfectly to reflect Him in a specific way. We were meant to be different! Nor are we created to *do* everything.

In the *Introduction,* I wrote in-depth about self-love. As a reminder, I said:

> Self-love is a gentle acceptance, and unconditional sense of support and caring, and a core of compassion for yourself. It is an abiding willingness to meet your own needs, allow yourself to feel and think whatever you feel and think, and see yourself as essentially worthy, good, valuable, and belonging in the world, deserving of happiness. And, most importantly, you believe you are ENOUGH, as you are. Self- love is developed early in life, and if childhood experiences damage our sense of self significantly, a lack of self-love can hurt us for a lifetime.

Folks who struggle with self-love don't believe they are ENOUGH. No matter how hard they try or how often they hear it from others, they can't seem to believe they are good enough.

A few of the more common characteristics of genuinely low self-esteem are:

- Struggle with anger or depression.
- Easy frustration.
- Eating disorders.
- Social withdraw.
- An inability to see yourself *squarely* or to be fair to yourself.
- Can't accept compliments.
- Self-neglect.
- Treat others well but yourself badly.
- Reluctant to take on challenges.

- Reluctant to put yourself first.

- Reluctant to trust your own opinion.

- Low life expectations for yourself.

Self-esteem is important for many reasons. We need to have a healthy self-esteem because it affects every aspect of our lives. Having a good self-esteem is essential, because:

- Without it, we can crumble and not show up for our life.

- It helps us feel good about ourselves.

- It gives us courage to try new things.

- It helps us honor and respect ourselves, even when we make mistakes.

- It encourages us to make healthy decisions for our minds and bodies.

This does not mean that people with good self-esteem discounts others. Instead, they value themselves and ensure their own feelings or needs are not discounted.

In this chapter, I'd like you to decide for yourself, once and for all, that you are ENOUGH. That's it. ENOUGH. Perfectly imperfect. Take the pressure off yourself and feel that in your body for a moment. What comes up for you? How does that feel?

Rocking what you've got is SELF-LOVE at its finest! It's about embracing yourself as you are in this moment. Knowing you are ENOUGH. Loving all of you, even if your body doesn't look like OR act like what you think it should. It's about reminding yourself you are worthy and dressing your best each day to reflect your worthiness.

It starts with a mindset of ENOUGH. Choose ENOUGH instead of punishing yourself with words that put you in a deeper, darker mood and tearing yourself down physically, emotionally and spiritually. I'm encouraging you to be gentle and loving to yourself.

For whatever traumatic reasons, I became disconnected from my body very early in life. Even as young as eight years old, I remember hating my body and wishing I had a different one. I didn't feel loved or that I belonged in my family or anywhere, frankly. Being disconnected also showed up in my life over the years as stress, overwhelm, a sense of emptiness, lack of meaning or purpose, and feeling uncertain about myself.

My inner critic continued to add fuel to the fire. Sad to say, *I am not enough* became my new inner mantra. I grew up with a beautiful dresser and mirror set in my bedroom. But you wouldn't really have known it. I covered the mirror in cardboard so I didn't have to look at myself. That's how much I loathed looking at myself in the mirror. I wished I was a different person, different size, different hair, different everything. I didn't believe I was enough. It took years before I was able to take the cardboard down and actually appreciate my body.

Some days, *Rock What You've Got* is still a tough one for me. When I walk on the beach, there are many gals with beautiful buff bodies passing by me. They are probably thirty years younger than me in their itsy-bitsy bikinis. I know I shouldn't compare myself to others. I try hard not to, but, I'm human. In the past, I would have verbally berated myself, which made me feel even worse. Nowadays, I embrace my beautiful body and appreciate what it does for me every day.

I encourage you to appreciate who you are right now. Know you are ENOUGH. Right here. Right now. You don't have to be someone you are not. Be the best version of YOU. Rock What You've Got is about accepting and loving the body and all of who you are or have in this moment. And, when you love who you are in this moment, you naturally begin to dress to reflect that beautiful inner you and feel rockin'.

Recently a coach of mine was getting ready to present at a conference. She dressed in a beautiful AND comfortable gown — her tummy wasn't squashed in Spanx! Her best friend helped her get dressed and said something like, "You're not going to go out there like THAT, are you?" My coach KNEW she was ENOUGH deep inside and she said, "Yes, I am. Just like this. I'm going out there." And, she did. And proceeded to teach many other women a powerful lesson: We may not look exactly how we want to look, but we are all masterpieces and beautiful, exactly how we are. Love every inch of yourself, no matter what. *Rock What You've Got*, make the best of it and be proud. Those were what I gleaned from her actions.

That coach, Liana Chaouli, in her recent book, *You are a Masterpiece: How to Dress a More Powerful and Authentic You*, teaches how to create a closet filled with tools to support your purpose, personality, and authenticity. She says:

> *Your wardrobe should lift you up, not beat you up. Just the thought of opening that closet door can ruin your day because the unconscious narrative will launch itself. "I'm too fat. I'm not good enough. I'm a failure." Remember you are a Masterpiece just the way you are and all of who you are is a blessed song...a song that the world needs in order to play this perfect symphony called life.*

Liana encourages men and women to "make it a practice to 'see yourself', not to look at, but truly see what is there and honor your 'Be-YOU-ti-FULL' self by bringing out your own natural colors through the colors you choose to wear." She challenges readers, asking, "What are you hiding and not allowing the world to see? What are you choosing to keep small inside your spirit? What are you NOT unleashing for fear of rejection? Write it down. Speak it out loud, and set it free... and notice the blossoming!"

Her mission is to further and support self-acceptance, self-esteem, and self-understanding in her clients from all walks of life. Her goal has always been to empower people through knowledge. Liana also adds:

I believe each human being is a Masterpiece. I believe that we are all works of genius created by the same awesome force which designed mountains and hummingbirds, the stars, and the twinkle in our eyes. And, I believe that we are constantly growing into the newest version of who we are called to be.

She encourages us to focus on our assets because it is empowering. The more your thoughts are in appreciation, the more you draw positive things to you.

A friend of mine had heard me talking about Rock What You've Got. One day when she was getting dressed, she started feeling bad about herself and her body when the words Rock What You've Got popped into her head. She told me later that when that happened, it helped her reset to a whole new outlook that perked her up. She ended up having a great day, partly because she reset her self-perspective.

In the next chapter, we're going to be talking about Making Friends with Your Kitchen. Keeping the components of your life working together starts in the kitchen with your fuel and helps you seamlessly step into the Limitless Soul that you are. All of these items are a reflection, though, of knowing you are ENOUGH.

Next time you're feeling down about your body, like my friend above, remember the words *Rock What You've Got* and do a mental reset. This quick reminder will fill your soul with the message that you are enough and allow you to show up in the world honoring and radiating who you truly are. And, that's the best version of YOU. My journal entries reflect that new me as well.

Dear Body:

Thank you for hanging in there with me. I love you. I honor you. I respect you. I appreciate you and your strength. You are resilient, patient, and beautiful! You are exactly who God created you to be. I see you. I hear you. I am listening.

Now it's your turn

Rock What You've Got

This might be the most difficult part of your journey: loving and accepting your beautiful body where it is today.

- Vow to stop beating yourself up with words that tear you down.

- Be gentle and kind to yourself, always.

- Appreciate yourself where you are, right in this moment.

- Write down all the ways in which you are thankful for your body.

- Love yourself unconditionally.

- Sort through your clothing, donating anything that doesn't fit or make you feel amazing.

- If you're inclined, work with a personal stylist to design outfits from your closet.

- Allow yourself to be seen and unleash your magnificence.

- If fears of rejection surface, pull out your journal and write them down.

- Take care of yourself by scheduling appointments with caregivers who support you.

- Repeat: **I am Enough**.

Make Friends With Your Kitchen

"Let food be thy medicine and medicine be thy food."

– Hippocrates

Kitchens. Food. Love. Those words tend to go together, either consciously or subconsciously. Due to its typically central location, the kitchen has been called the heart of the home. Family members and guests gather in this space to greet one another, laugh, cry, and prepare meals that are shared in a space of love.

We pour ourselves into the food on a daily basis. Cutting, slicing, and dicing food to nourish your own loved ones. As you prepare, you are unconsciously pouring your own love into the food that your family will digest. If a family isn't getting along, the kitchen can become a place of anger and unrest. Fast food meals heated on high in the microwave become a blaring reality, mirroring their life of anger and emptiness. Although I personally love to cook healthy fresh foods, the kitchen was a source of great pain and anguish in years past. In previous journals, I even called the kitchen POISON. As you read in the *Rock What You've Got* chapter, loving my body wasn't exactly on the top of my list each day! My grandparents would weigh and measure us any chance they could while marking it on a closet door for all to see. Although meant for fun and to show the grandchildren growing, it became quite a sore spot for me, fueling my inadequate feelings.

I suspect if you're drawn to this book, you are a very busy person who may be a little confused by what your kitchen offers you. The fuel you are putting into your body may not be helping you to feel your best and to live your best life. You most likely are the person who is planning, shopping, and preparing the meals for the household, too. What you do or don't do affects not only you but others in the household and guests. In a way, you provide the fuel the rest of the family runs on.

What you eat either dumbs you down or lifts you up. It can decrease your energy, pull you into a deeper depression, or encourage you to rise higher. Yes, your choice of food does all of that!

According to a National Center of Health Statistics 2003 survey, about 65.2% of American adults are overweight or obese as a result of poor nutrition. Being overweight puts people at risk for developing a host of disorders and conditions, some of them life- threatening. Poor eating (overeating, undereating, or malnutrition) can lead to a host of issues including but not limited to: high cholesterol, heart disease, diabetes, stroke, gout, cancer, compromised immune system, hair, and teeth and skin problems.

Anything you can do to help facilitate healing for your body, mind, and soul should be considered. Begin with your nutrition if you're feeling any of the following: depression, anxiety, low energy, extreme fatigue, dry brittle hair, diarrhea, apathy, lack of appetite, or sweets cravings.

According to the National Eating Disorders Association (NEDA):

Eating disorders are serious, life-threatening illnesses that impact millions of people every year in the United States.

Eating disorders are real, complex, and devastating conditions that can have serious consequences for health, productivity, and relationships. They are not a fad, phase or lifestyle choice. Eating disorders are serious, potentially life-threatening conditions that affect a person's emotional and physical health.

People struggling with an eating disorder need to seek professional help. The earlier a person with an eating disorder seeks treatment, the greater the likelihood of physical and emotional recovery.

In the United States, twenty million women and ten million men suffer from a clinically significant eating disorder at some time in their life. By age six, girls especially start to express concerns about their own weight or shape. About 40% to 60% of elementary school girls (ages six to twelve) are concerned about their weight, or about becoming too fat. This concern endures through life [Smolak, 2011].

Here are a few of the popular ways we abuse food:

- **Anorexia Nervosa** – inadequate food intake leading to a weight that is clearly too low.

- **Binge Eating Disorder** – frequent episodes of consuming very large amounts of food but without behaviors to prevent weight gain, such as self-induced vomiting.

- **Bulimia Nervosa** – frequent episodes of consuming very large amounts of food followed by behaviors to prevent weight gain, such as self-induced vomiting.

At one time or another I suffered from several of these eating disorders, beginning in early grade school. Nothing ever worked to heal the disorders until I began looking at the root cause, which was low self-esteem or low self-worth. For me, the kitchen represented a place of stress and disconnect.

Obviously, I had to eat but I was divided as to the best way to go about fueling my body and staying slim. Often I would not eat at all. Days would go by without any food except a cup of soup. My body would be starving and demand food, sending me into overeating to balance out the unintentional neglect. This cycle continued until my late 20s.

A few years back, I devoured the book *A Course in Weight Loss: 21 Spiritual Lessons for Surrendering Your Weight Forever* by Marianne Williamson. This book was an integral catalyst for helping me to heal the disconnection between food, my body and my soul. In it Marianne writes:

> *Your true self is programmed perfectly by nature to think and behave in ways that are healthy and strong. Your job now is not only to disconnect from the matrix of addiction or compulsion, but also to reconnect with the matrix of perfection in which you were created and in which your spirit remains. This matrix of perfection is the real you. The real you is already perfect, in every aspect and in every way. You are not the problem, because you are divinely perfect.*

Food was one of the very first areas where I changed my life. I'd always been interested in nutrition and eating healthy but when I finally committed to properly nourishing my body, I noticed an increased quality in my life. Everyone has their own meaning of what healthy eating is. Mine is eating the appropriate amount of nutrition that my body needed – not too much and not too little. Enough to nourish and fuel my activities.

As I began the steps I have outlined in this book along with those in Marianne's book, issues that had plagued me for decades faded away! This success has not been without much hard work — physically, emotionally and spiritually — as well as working with various counselors, nutritionists, and coaches. Thankfully, I am free from all descriptive eating disorders and enjoy my life, freely eating that which nourishes and heals my body.

I encourage you in this chapter to *Make Friends with Your Kitchen*. That may sound odd, but I really want you to enjoy your space and what you do there! It's important to enjoy the preparing, cooking and eating of food that nourishes you. Slow down, taste, smell, enjoy! It's a room in the house where we spend a lot of time and if it's not serving you well and making you feel awesome then there needs to be some adjustments.

Sit in your kitchen space. How does it feel to you? Does it need to be organized? Cleaned top to bottom? Write down what it needs so that it can be a space that feels good to you. Think about what utensils you need so that you can cook your healthy meals in this sacred place.

Next, consider your own personal nutrition. Write down what you are eating for two weeks straight, and then examine it closely. Make sure to include what you ate, what time, and how you felt (physically and emotionally) before and after.

Ask yourself these questions:

- Did I eat some protein first thing in the morning?

- How do I feel after lunch? Tired or energized?

- Do I get an afternoon slump and crave sweets?

- How much processed food am I eating?

- Am I eating out too much or should I consider cooking more at home?

- Am I eating when I'm truly hungry or do I eat to fill another

- need?

- Am I eating too many breads or other carbohydrates?

- These are a few questions you should ask yourself as you examine your meal plan after a couple of weeks.

My good friend and Integrative Nutrition Coach, Laurie Runyan (HealingLuv.com), loves to reference her cooking space as *The Healing Kitchen.*

I also love how the authors at The HealingKitchen describe what *The Healing Kitchen* means to them:

> *The Healing Kitchen is a place where healing begins. It's where the "Cure is in the Cupboard" and Food is used as medicine.*

> *In our family, the kitchen has always been the center of our home. It's where we play card games, discuss world issues, learn about relationship building, and prepare and enjoy good food.*

> *It's the most trafficked room in our house. We share intimate conversation, resolve conflicts, and experience educational moments. Most importantly, it offers my family a place to come to heal and re-energize.*

A kitchen that accomplishes all these things is naturally a healing place to be. It attracts people to it and creates harmony and balance to those working in it. It is inviting, peaceful and soothing and so it should be, after all, it's the place where you prepare food: food your body needs to sustain and maintain its present level of health and if necessary, heal itself.

Mostly importantly, as you are considering whether you should eat something, hold it, smell it, pray over it. For example, as a test, next time you are hungry, hold an apple. Ask yourself if this apple would give you energy. Feel how your body responds to that apple.

Secondly, hold a Twinkie or another processed food available in your pantry. Ask yourself if this Twinkie would give you the energy you need. See again how your body responds. Which feels better to you—the apple or the Twinkie? Which one would give you the nutrition and energy your body needs? Which food item would nourish you physically?

Sometimes we get confused with seeking physical nourishment (eating) when what we really need is emotional or spiritual nourishment. Do consider that as well as you are deciding what to eat. Maybe you're not truly hungry at all, but instead need a hug!

I know this may frustrate you, but I'm not going to give you a diet to follow! Every BODY is different and has different needs for nourishment. As I will discuss in the chapter on Taking Charge, I've adopted a unique meal plan to facilitate healing of my thyroid, adrenals, and other hormones. I highly recommend working with an expert in the area of nutrition. You won't be disappointed!

That being said, my best advice for every BODY is this:

1. If you can't pronounce it, don't eat it!

2. Consider cutting the wheat out of your diet.

3. Shop for groceries one to two times a week. As soon as you get home, prepare vegetables so they are ready to go. Cook any food items ahead for the week too.

Integrative Registered Dietitian Nutritionist and Health Coach, Carmina McGee (CarminaMcGee.com), offers some great advice to you as well:

Our kitchens are often the hearts of our home. Just as our hearts need tending, so do our kitchens, so in turn they can become spaces that nourish us.

Let your kitchen become your ally in creating a healthier you. Here are some simple strategies to help you get started:

1. *Create a supportive environment by clearing out all known trigger foods that entice you into eating in a way that sabotages your health (you know what they are).*

2. *Stock your refrigerator and pantry with a wide variety of delicious, colorful, real foods. The kind grown on a farm, whole or minimally processed, not manufactured in a food lab. Choose fresh, organic vegetables and fruits, nuts and seeds, beans, whole grains and lean protein sources (poultry, fish, lean red meats, game meats).*

3. *Be kind to your bones and organs, especially your kidneys. Nix the soft drinks (yes, even diet ones), excess caffeine and sports drinks. Re-create a spa atmosphere by making refreshing pitchers of filtered water infused with fresh whole berries, citrus and*

cucumber slices, sprigs of mint and drink to your heart's delight.

4. *Always have some truly amazing dark chocolate on hand, the best you can find where you allow a square or two to slowly melt in your mouth, something in the 70% cacao range. Savor the taste — it takes very little to experience that little bit of bliss that is very health-giving.*

So open your heart, feed your body and really start living.

As I implemented these solutions above, my mind became clearer and the mask of low self-esteem began melting away. My mood improved tremendously, depression lifted, energy increased, and an overall expanded quality of life prevailed.

Ann works full time, has four children at home, and prepares most of the family meals. Overcome with low energy and in need of assistance organizing her meals, she made friends with her kitchen, instead of the drive-through, which she used to hit on her way home from work. After we talked, Ann began planning ahead, knowing what she'd purchase at the grocery store the day before she went shopping. By purchasing and preparing, she knew when she walked into her house each evening what food was ready to go for dinner. Meals became easier for her and no longer a source of stress. It saved her family quite a bit of money and they all began feeling quite energized because the meals were more nutrient dense.

Another client, Michael, had a different challenge. Michael struggled with afternoon sugar cravings. When we reviewed his two week food plan, it became clear he wasn't getting the proper nutrition in the morning (a balance of protein, fats, and carbs) that would set him up for a sugar-free afternoon. Michael began preparing eggs, greens, and veggies with olive oil and gluten free toast each morning. Almost immediately, his afternoon cravings dissipated, mental clarity returned and his overall energy increased.

Then there was Karen, who had a history of eating disorders that kept her in fear of her own kitchen. She would scurry in and out as fast as she could, preparing and eating as fast as she could, to avoid feel anything while she was there. I asked her to sit in her kitchen with a notepad. Write down what came up as she sat there. And, kept writing. She went deep and then, deeper. She wrote that the kitchen was her enemy, reminding her of a childhood home full of anger and fighting. The kitchen reverberated with loud voices. As a result, her kitchen didn't feel like a place of love. Instead it felt burdensome, angry, and overwhelming at times.

Subconsciously and unnoticed to her, these feelings would come up for her every time she entered her own kitchen. Only once she sat down in it and let her memories and feelings rise was she able to acknowledge and feel her pain, and release it. This also is what I described in the Being Still chapter on feeling your feelings. Since working deeply in this area, Karen has transformed how she reacts in her kitchen and around food. She now enjoys preparing and savoring her meals in her kitchen, which now feels like a space of love.

You too can transform your relationship to your kitchen and food! As you choose to purchase, prepare, and eat higher energy foods, you and your family will have more energy and gain mental clarity. Sugar cravings will disappear. You will begin to feel better physically and emotionally. Dry skin will disappear and you will glow! Meals will be a breeze to prepare on a moment's notice. You will save money by not eating out. And, you will feel fabulous!

As you feel more comfortable in your own kitchen space, eating true food that nourishes your body and soul, you will naturally draw to yourself a team of support and a family of love. We will be discussing this in the very next chapter. In the meantime, look at your own healing kitchen and what is produced in it as a friend, not a foe. Bless it and allow it to nourish you from the inside, out.

Now it's your turn

Make Friends with Your Kitchen

- Commit to nurturing your body with healthy foods.
- Be mindful when eating: smell, taste, and savor what you eat.
- Eat slowly.
- Keep a food journal for two weeks, noting how you feel after eating each meal.
    - Are you eating protein first thing in the morning?
    - How much processed sugar is in your diet?
    - When and how much do you consume of carbohydrates and breads?
    - After lunch, do you feel energized or depleted?
    - Do you have an afternoon slump?
    - Do you have sweets cravings?
    - How often do you eat out?
    - Do you eat until you are no longer hungry or stop when you're full?
- Reduce or eliminate those things from your diet which don't increase your energy. Get rid of your trigger foods.
- Determine what portion sizes are right for you.
- Stock your kitchen with colorful, fresh food.
- Sit in your kitchen. How does it feel? What memories can you evoke? Write your thoughts and reflections in your journal.
- Is your kitchen organized? If not, schedule time to organize it (or hire a professional organizer).
- Eliminate from your diet foods with ingredients you can't pronounce.
- Create a weekly menu and write down what you need on a grocery list; buy only what you need. Shop at least once per week.

- Vary your menu with the seasons, using fresh fruits and vegetables.
- Create spa water by filling a pitcher with fresh water and sliced cucumbers, or berries and sage or citrus.

Additional Resources

- *In Defense of Food* by Michael Pollan

Who's in Your Tribe?

"If you want to go fast, go alone. If you want to go far, go together."

– African Proverb

I'm sure, like me, when you think of the word tribe all kinds of images come to mind. Maybe even a group of people dressed like Indians circling a massive bonfire, chanting! Although the image may be a tad outdated, the purpose of a tribe in today's world still holds true. We all need a group of like-minded, supportive people around us. The first layer closest to us in our tribe should be our loved ones. We need to surround ourselves on a daily basis with these folks who support us. And, I mean deliberately choose. On purpose, you need to seek love, as well as be open to receiving love when it shows up at your door.

I had a friend tell me once it was difficult to show love to me. She was right. I had erected a wall around myself as protection for potential hurt. I found it easy to give to others but the door only opened one way. I didn't let it become a revolving door. Today, I try to be conscious so that my generous giving doesn't deplete me, and I am open to receiving the gifts of love others have for me.

After our loved ones, the next layers of our tribe can be other friends, mentors, and coaches you seek for support in a specific area or even health care professionals (see Take Charge chapter for more information on this specific team of support). When I began working with a coach, I was always surprised when asked, "Who is supporting you? Who is helping you on a day-to-day basis?"

Speechless, I hadn't considered that I needed someone to lean on! I lived by myself, newly divorced, as an entrepreneur and an empty nester. I did feel like an island castaway most days! I needed people in my life who understood me and who saw me. I needed to be surrounded by men and women who could help me maneuver the road less taken.

Just like we hire exercise trainers, we can hire coaches for about every area of our lives including life, business, health, nutrition, organization and time management. There are even more specific niches within each of the categories above. You name it; it's probably available somewhere! Do not ever feel like you have to go through life alone!

We are meant to collaborate and be in a tribe together. Make it a priority to find like-minded folks who you enjoy being with.

When I was a stay-at-home mom of preschoolers, it was pretty easy to find a moms' groups at our local churches. However, when my youngest son entered kindergarten, I was kicked out of Mothers of Preschoolers! (Not really, but their focus is for moms with children not yet in school.) I still needed a tribe of other moms, so I joined with a couple other ladies from our own church and started Mom2Mom. We focused on moms with children from birth to high school age. Sometimes our meetings would have 50 moms in attendance and at least the same number of kids.

It was great fun building a tribe of women who were like-minded and devoted to supporting one another. These women were my co-pilots through those years of navigating the mommy roadways. (It's thrilling for me to know that even decades later, this Mom2Mom group is still going strong.)

When I returned to work from home, my available time shrank and I struggled to fit in the right group. I was alone at home and had little time to venture out and find a new tribe. This predates the popular MeetUps. Any extra time I had was spent volunteering at the kids' functions, which doubled as my outlet for adult interaction. Although the volunteer groups gave me a nest to relax in, it wasn't exactly supportive on the deeper level for my day-to-day challenges that I encountered as a stay-at-home mom entrepreneur.

After my divorce, I gradually began building a team of support. I wasn't very good at asking for help, but I had to learn to ask anyway. If they said "no," it was okay. I no longer took it personally, but I needed to at least ask. My new support group included friends, family, doctors, nutrition experts, a finance manager, an accountant, a bookkeeper, a VA (Virtual Assistant), help keeping up with the family home (until it sold), a business mastermind group, and a book coach.

On the days that work brought my clients in virtually, I made it a point to venture out of my office to a yoga class or to meet with friends for a walk or a cup of coffee. It was too tempting for me to get all settled in for days at a time. Although I enjoy the quiet, when I'm around like-minded people, my tribe, I am nourished on the inside.

When I look at my life now compared to even a year ago, I am surrounded by a strong tribe in layers of support that cannot be easily broken. Their love and endless support for my crazy wild life, while encouraging me to keep shooting for the moon, fills my heart. Finding this tribe didn't happen by accident. I deliberately began seeking those who would assist me and had to allow others to leave my life, as painful as that was.

If you realize that your *tribe* could be a little tighter or more supportive, begin to journal about your own values and dreams. This will help you get clarity on your like-minded tribe folks. Ask yourself questions like I did:

- Who or what kind of person do I need to add into my life to help support me? Where am I lacking that someone else can help me?

- Who's on my team?

- Who supports me?

- Which loved ones surround me on a daily basis?

- Do I need a cleaning lady?

- Do I need help mowing my yard?

- Do I need someone to help me get organized?

- Do I need an exercise trainer?

- Do I need a health and nutrition coach?

- Do I need someone to check on the house while I'm away?

- Do I need to join Toastmasters to practice speaking?

- Do I need a book coach to keep me on track with writing?

- How can I connect with a friend today?

- Are there any Meet Ups in my area I could attend?

- What support in my business do I need?

In what areas are you struggling? Look at those areas and see where you could use some support. Don't be shy about reaching out.

Let down your guard to allow love and support into your heart. I realize if you've been hurt, as most of us have, then this can be scary. Sometimes we have to move through the fear into love. As I allowed myself to begin to love again, it started with ME. Not a selfish kind of LOVE, a kind of self-love that honored me, as described in the *Introduction* of this book. As I started to appreciate who I was created to be, I was better able to let others into my life who could love and support me. These people were folks that I deliberately set out to bring into my life. They became my team of support.

You, as well, can begin expanding your tribe (love and support) and benefit from the increased nourishment that it brings. The African proverb says, "If you want to go fast, go alone. If you want to go far, go together." Being a part of a tribe will allow you to feel loved and supported. It will also challenge you to grow into the best version of yourself. Take responsibility now for who you are, your values, and your beliefs and watch your tribe expand! In the next chapter, you will take those same values and apply them to taking charge of your life and your health.

In the meantime, get crystal clear on your own values and who you are. As you do that, you will naturally attract those folks who seek to do life with you.

Now it's your turn

Who's in Your Tribe

Rachel Wolchin wrote, "Surround yourself with people that reflect who you want to be and how you want to feel. Energies are contagious."

It's time to ask yourself:

- Who or what kind of person do I need to add to my life to help support me?

- Who is on my team?

- Who supports me? Who doesn't?

- Which loved ones surround you on a daily basis?

- Do you have any friends who, when their name appears on your caller ID, you let it go to voicemail? Why?

- Look at your life and the one you're building. Ask yourself if the following support would benefit you:

  - Cleaning service

  - Personal trainer

  - Professional organizer

  - Lawn care professional

  - Health and nutrition coach

  - Housesitter/Petsitter

  - Virtual Assistant

  - Book coach

  - Speaking coach/program

- Look at your business and determine where you can delegate so you can work in your areas of excellence.

take Charge

"When you take charge of your life, there is no longer need to ask permission of other people or society at large. When you ask permission, you give someone veto power over your life."

– Geoffrey F. Abert

Only YOU are in charge of YOU, your health, and your life. No one else. Not your spouse, not your children, and not your doctors. This means that you have to take full responsibility for your life — physically, emotionally, and spiritually. Steve Maraboli says, "Start walking your own walk. This journey is YOURS. Take charge of it. Stop giving other people your power to shape your life."

You get to create the life you desire. No longer does your past have to weigh you down.

Would you say you are running your own life? Are others walking over your plans?

How's your health? Are you feeling listless, depressed, lethargic, frustrated, or angry?

I totally get it. I allowed others, even my children's schedules, to run my life for many, many years. Everyone else's demands and needs were put before my own. I own it. I completely allowed it. At the time, I didn't know I could do something different. Now, I do, and now, I do things differently. You can, too!

I want to encourage you today to Take Charge of your life and health.

No one else can do this for you.

– Take Charge of your Health –

As I've mentioned in the *Introduction*, depression plagued me on and off over the years. Often I felt listless and even unable to cry out for help. On occasions, I had thoughts of suicide. Although I didn't want to take pharmaceuticals, it became a medical necessity. My doctor and good friend helped and guided as best she could.

One morning, I loaded the kids into my new minivan for a quick drop-off to grade school. But, strangely, my new van wouldn't start. Nothing. Almost immediately frustration rose inside me. My children watched in horror as my head repeatedly hit the steering wheel and window. I had a seizure causing my body to shake and jump uncontrollably. Thirty minutes later, I awoke in the house, vomiting. My seizure was a reaction to a prescription antidepressant.

As I look back at that episode, I see it was a turning point in my life. It was clear to me immediately that God and his angels protected us that day by not allowing the van to start. Had I ventured out on the road even thirty seconds later and then had the seizure, we probably would have ended up in the community retention pond. I am ever thankful to the Heavens for help that day. Fear for my life and my children's lives became the catalyst to get well.

I've heard it said, "The greatest wealth is health." I do believe this— wholeheartedly. Health can be described as the general condition of the body or mind with reference to soundness and vigor. Isn't that what we all seek? A thyroid/adrenal nutrition expert, one of my nutrition mentors and a bundle of energy, Andrea Beaman, wrote in her latest book, *Health is Wealth: Make a Delicious Investment in You*, "Health is wealth literally means it's possible to have a rich life without compromising ourselves in the process. We need to learn to invest in our health on a daily basis."

Last winter, Andrea coached me through a difficult period, assisting me to heal my thyroid and adrenal issues. Although we laid a fabulous foundation for nutritional healing, I was most surprised by her focus on self-love. Her encouragement to be gentle with myself and practice self-love allowed me to *Take Charge* of my health in a loving and kind way.

Here is some *Take Charge* Advice from Andrea Beaman:

> *We all have an innate healing wisdom that lives within us. I often hear it when clients sign up for health coaching.*
>
> *During a session they'll say, "I know I need to eat better, I know I need daily exercise, I know I need to quit my job, I know I need to end my dead-end relationship, I know..."*

Most of us know exactly what we need to do to help ourselves, but we don't take action on it.

Why not?

I believe it's because we haven't been taught to make our self and our health our number one priority, and to understand that we are responsible for our life.

Self-care is not on the agenda at our schools and it's not taught in our homes or workplace. So where the heck are we supposed to learn this valuable information?

For me, experience was the best teacher. I learned about self-care and the body's natural ability to heal through my own sickness. I was programmed dysfunctionally like many other humans on this planet, to wait until disease came and knocked me to the floor before I made an effort to do something.

The "something" I did was not recommended by my doctors. It was considered radical and unconventional. Within fourteen days of taking responsibility for my health and incorporating self-care, I noticed improvements; clear skin, better sleep, regular bowel movements, and increased energy. Very quickly, I made the connection that within me lives an innate healing power. All I had to do was nourish it with the proper physical, emotional and spiritual food it needed to thrive.

It's been over sixteen years since making that initial commitment to self-care, and today my vibrant health (as well as the health of many clients and students) is proof that Thyroid disease, and other diseases, is curable.

The ability to heal an imbalanced or diseased condition takes patience, persistence and hard work, but you are worth it. It's time we learned how to put our health first and incorporate self-care as an option for our health-care.

Here are some simple steps to activating your body's innate healing wisdom:

STEP ONE *– Take responsibility for your illness. This may sound harsh, but whatever the condition is, own it. It is yours.*

STEP TWO *– Become aware of your physical body and notice how it "feels" on a daily basis:*

- *Is it aching?*
- *Is your skin irritated?*
- *Do you have vibrant energy?*
- *Are you struggling to get through the day?*
- *Are you sleeping well?*
- *Is your digestive system functioning properly?*

If your body is not functioning properly it's time for serious self-care. Hire a health coach for gosh sakes!

STEP THREE *– Eat clean and get off the crap! Our daily food becomes our cells, our blood, our organs, our body,* *and our mind. We are what we eat. And, I mean that literally! If we eat food filled with indigestible chemical substances that impair the immune system, we cannot create vibrant health. Stop spending money on health-care that doesn't create health and put your money where your mouth is. Purchase local, seasonal food that is naturally grown and lovingly prepared. It's as simple, and as hard, as that.*

STEP FOUR – After getting "clean" dig deeper into the emotional body (the chakras). It's here you can begin recognizing behavior patterns that may or may not be health-supportive. It's time to discover who you are and what your relationship is to the world around you. If I had simply changed my diet and my lifestyle, without working on my emotional body, self-healing may not have been quite as effective.

STEP FIVE – Incorporate ancient healing techniques or use any modern healing practice that works with the body, mind, and spirit, not against it. Some healing methods I use include acupuncture, massage, reflexology, aromatherapy, chiropractic, shamanic drumming, chanting, chakra healing, meditation, and many others.

Of course, there are many more steps to healing, but these are the basics. Remember, as long as you are alive and breathing you can improve any condition. When we become aware of our situation and take full responsibility for what we have created, we can flip the switch from disease – promoting to self-healing at any time.

Your body is a true masterpiece made with the beautiful yarn of hormones holding together an intricate tapestry. If one yarn or hormone is off-balance, the others are pulled out of place, as well. Sometimes, we don't even realize we are experiencing declining health from unbalanced hormones until we hit a wall. This is true for men and women alike.

If you do not feel well, get help. Get help NOW! You do not have to feel this way. You do not have to be miserable the rest of your life. Although I'm not a huge proponent of taking prescription medicine, I adjusted my thinking in order to get myself well. I encourage you as well to be open-minded about your own situation.

There are times in our lives where it seems we are not emotionally strong enough to handle whatever we're given. For years, I ignored many ill-health symptoms of thyroid disease that I should have sought help for long before I did. Honestly, even though my physician (bless her) would tell me my numbers were off, I couldn't sustain taking care of myself. My home roiled with turmoil and I didn't want to take pharmaceuticals. I believed if I ignored the lab reports, the issue would go away.

Well, the issues didn't go away and today I'm facing even worse health issues than if I had handled things when they came up years ago. But, I wasn't ready to face my health challenges. I wasn't ready to take responsibility. I was depressed and worried if I was even going to make it through the day. I really didn't care if my thyroid numbers were off. I didn't understand that much of the readings were related to how I was living my life and not loving myself.

Frustration of being sick, I felt overwhelmed yet I refused the help right in front of me. And there is ALWAYS help right around you, starting with your family doctor, any doctor. Get tests run that relate to your symptoms. Study, do your own research. Keep looking until you know exactly what's going on inside of you and what you need to do about it.

An abundance of assistance is available to help you feel better if you are willing to put in the work. You may need a quick visit to your family doctor to get things rolling or, like me, you may need an entire team (physicians, specialists, nurse practitioners, acupuncturist and nutritionist) of support! Find the group you trust and partner together with them to benefit your health. Most importantly, make sure your team knows what each is recommending and prescribing.

Bottom line: you are in charge. It's your body and your decision what you take or don't take. If something doesn't feel right, pay attention to this feeling. Take action to make it feel right. You may even have to replace a team member or two. There is no room for egos when it comes to your body and your health.

Your quality of life depends on doing this work. Do not delay! You cannot expect someone else to do this work for you. Work with your team in order to make the best decisions for YOU. Every BODY is different. Ramp up your nutrition in the healing kitchen (see chapter titled *Make Friends with Your Kitchen*), get your hormone levels checked, and other appropriate medical tests, meditate, exercise, and add on the appropriate supplements and medicines to assist in your healing.

Everyone knows they ought to work-out more or eat better. I challenge you to step up your workout one notch. If you're currently working out three days a week—increase it to four. If you're eating a healthy breakfast, add in a nutritious lunch, one that will support you through an afternoon without sugar cravings. And, believe me you can live a life without sugar cravings!

– Take Charge of Your Life –

We need to *Take Charge* of our health, our life, and our wealth. One area affects the other. Taking charge in one arena can catapult the other areas or, if left to the world at large, reduce them to rubble.

You can feel better. You can work smarter, not longer. You can have your health and wealth. You can have it all!

There are many areas in which you can *Take Charge* of your life, such as:

- Thinking, beliefs, and mindset.
- *Sleep, Schedules, and Surroundings.*
- Nutrition, health, and fitness.
- Finances.
- Personal boundaries.
- Self-love and self-care.
- Relationships in all areas of your life.

In the *Sleep, Schedules, and Surroundings* chapter, we discussed in- depth about the importance of sleep, schedules and your surroundings. In the previous chapter, we focused on making friends with your kitchen and improving your nutrition. In the chapter *Silence the Mind Chatter*, we focused on your thinking and how to silence endless mind chatter. It's vitally important that you realize that you are in charge. You — not your spouse and not your children. This is your life. You are responsible for you. You are also responsible for teaching others how to treat you.

TV personality, author, and psychologist Dr. Philip McGraw, often says, "You teach people how to treat you." Early on in my marriage I couldn't even ask my ex-husband to return a video (back in the days when we rented VHS/DVDs from movie stores). For whatever reason, I had trouble asking for help even for little things. Because of that, he never thought I needed help, so none was offered. Until I realized that:

1. I need HELP.

2. I could ask for it.

3. He could offer assistance.

Part of not asking for help is also not taking a yes or no personally. That's a whole different book! Bottom line, I had to learn to ask for what I needed and to detach from my ex-husband's response.

If we aren't taking responsibility for ourselves, our actions, or our needs, then we most likely will feel like a victim. We may even resent others. (Do you see how everything in our lives is connected?) Our health is tied to how we take care of ourselves, which in turn affects our body and impacts how we feel and act. One of my fabulous business coaches, Baeth Davis, reminded me recently that men have the tendency to work (business) to feel good. For women, we can't work (business) very well when we don't feel good. Not feeling good impacts our capacity for quality work which results in decreased income (wealth).

Areas that we haven't yet covered in this book or chapter are taking charge of your finances, boundaries, and basic self-love practices.

– Finances –

People who know me well will laugh when they read that I'm writing about finances! Although I began as an accounting major in college, it didn't take long before I realized that numbers weren't my thing. Over the years I was married to a CPA, daily bookkeeping for our family wasn't in my hands. However, since my divorice, I've spent the last few years developing my own system of tracking investments, spending, and savings for myself, both personally and for my business. It has been incredibly rewarding and enjoyable to be in control of the funds that God has entrusted me with.

When I look at my bank accounts, whether they are low or high, plentiful or pitiful, I am thankful for the abundance. I know that with great wealth comes great responsibility—not only for myself and my family, but for the needs of the world God leads me to assist.

I encourage you as well to look at your bank balances daily. Thank God for the abundance in your checking and savings accounts. Even if it doesn't look like what you want, what you focus on will expand! Keep doing it anyway!

– Boundaries –

There were many days in the past when I allowed others to hijack my day's schedule. Obviously, this was a boundary issue for me! I wanted to keep everyone happy and keep peace at all cost. I believed it was what I was supposed to do and had to do. When I delved into my subconscious beliefs playing out in my life, I was stunned at how often I allowed others to control my schedule.

On days where my schedule was full, I might receive a phone call from a friend who needed me to watch her kids for a few hours.

"Sure," I would say. Then someone else needed help with a project. Could I help with that, too? "Sure," I would say. Oh wait! There's an emergency with one of my client's websites. The "emergency" turned out to be they wanted to change out a picture on their website, but it HAD to be done that day. "Sure," I would say. Rinse, wash, repeat.

I sacrificed myself to please others. I gave my time, talents, money, and energy to people whom I loved dearly, while neglecting myself. I knew intuitively something was wrong, but I didn't know what to do about it. I just thought this is who I am.

Examine your own boundaries. Do you have definite non-negotiable borders placed around certain areas? Keep in mind that we still need to be flexible for true emergencies guaranteed to pop up. Life is full of give and take moments. Even though I have a schedule, as I mentioned in Chapter 5, I'm still very open to where and what God is leading me to do.

– Loving Yourself –

It's time for you to *Take Charge* of loving yourself. If you can't love yourself, how do you expect others to love you fully? As mentioned in the Introduction, I couldn't even say the words, "self- love." The words made my stomach turn. I thought it utterly selfish and un-church-like to say I loved myself. I didn't believe I was enough. It didn't matter how many people told me I was, I couldn't believe them.

Folks who struggle with self-love don't believe they are ENOUGH. No matter how hard they try or how often they hear it from others, they can't seem to believe others' words. People with self- love issues may also talk a lot—usually about themselves—or seek out validation from others.

What I've learned on this journey so far, is that self-love is instrumental in propelling you forward into the life of your dreams. You must experience self-love to tap into your true soul's calling, not in a selfish way, but rather in a way that says, "I take responsibility for who I am." If you're just beginning this self-love journey, you will benefit greatly by the practices already mentioned in this book, such as being still, silencing the mind chatter, meditation, prayer, mindfulness, getting out in nature, lining up your support team, and making friends with your kitchen.

There are hundreds of ways you can begin loving yourself. Other examples may be:

- Mirror work made famous by Louise Hay.
- Inner child work.
- Dress for success.
- Talk and listen to your body.
- Drink lots of water.
- Releasing exercises.
- Create compassion.
- Work out.
- Let go of toxins in your life.

At LimitlessSoul.com, I offer private coaching services and VIP retreats, where I walk you through all of the specific areas outlined in this book, plus more on how to love yourself more fully. We work on cementing self-love practices into your daily life. I want you to know that you can change.

You have the power in your mind to propel yourself forward, if you so choose. No longer do you have to let your past affect your present and certainly not your future. You can create the life and business you desire. The perfect place to begin is taking charge of your health and your life.

When I began to Take Charge of my own life and health, my world took an expectedly pleasant turn. My depression, energy levels, and health skyrocketed to a level I hadn't experienced in years.

My mind was clear and my thoughts were focused. Sleep came easily, and I began to enjoy a full night's rest instead of three hours a night as I had in the past. I found it effortless to stick to a schedule and follow through on boundaries because I knew my focus. I controlled my finances, instead of the other way around.

I felt supported for the first time because of the team I surrounded myself with, as well as various regular self-love practices instilled in my life. Those practices allowed me to count on myself, not others, for permission to be happy.

Like me, a client, Elizabeth, allowed others to hijack her day all too often. She committed herself to a daily workout at 9 o'clock in the morning. However, it seemed she continually got asked to attend meetings or various appointments at that time. She disregarded commitments to herself and her health in trade for making others happy by meeting their expectations first.

I talked to Elizabeth about her self-love practice and protecting her time boundary to say she was unavailable at that particular time each day. (If you are struggling with self-love, a time boundary of a workout isn't important to you, so you let other people walk all over it.)

Elizabeth welcomed the opportunity for growth and began making it clear that she couldn't begin her morning meetings and errands until 10 o'clock in the morning. This was such a simple fix. However, for those of us who struggle with loving ourselves, we don't want to let others down. It's easy for us to give up commitments to ourselves because we don't think we deserve the commitment. Tackling this area was a huge growth opportunity for Elizabeth. With her new fixed boundary solidly in place, she occasionally had to tell others no. She felt empowered as her self-esteem increased with each exercise of this new boundary muscle and she quietly smiled with eagerness, loving her new self.

Depending on which areas you choose to *Take Charge* of in life, you could expect for yourself, all or some of the following results:

- Increased energy.
- Increased health.
- Feel more positive overall.
- Increased empowerment.
- Increased self-esteem.
- Feel more loving towards yourself and others.
- Less depression.
- Less frustration.
- Less anger.
- You can feel better.
- You can work smarter, not longer.
- You can have your health and wealth.
- Feel supported.
- Clear mind.

- Focused energy and thoughts.

- Sweet, deep sleep at night.

- Feel in control of life, health, and wealth.

By assuming responsibility for your life, health, finances, boundaries, and most especially loving yourself, you will have built a solid foundation. This rock solid core will assist you when life is teeter tottering. You will be able to withstand the movement to and fro explained in the next chapter, *Allowing What Is*.

Enjoy the process of taking charge of your life. No longer will you be asking others for permission to be happy! You can choose in this moment to be the joy that you seek.

Now it's your turn

Take Charge

Here are a few questions and prompts to help you evaluate how "in charge" of your own life you are:

- Here are areas where you can **Take Charge**:
    - Thinking and mindset
    - Sleep, Schedules, and Surroundings
    - Nutrition, health, and fitness
    - Finances
    - Personal boundaries
    - Self-love and self-care
    - Relationships

- How often to you schedule time for yourself only to sacrifice that time to others?

- Do you feel listless, depressed, lethargic, frustrated, or angry?

- Do you ever feel taken advantage of?

- Has your body revolted by sending illness or dysfunction your way? Take responsibility for your illness or dysfunction.

- Take a body inventory daily. Is your skin irritated? Do your muscles and joints ache? Where do you struggle during the day? What feels great? When are you most alert and active? How are you sleeping (quality and quantity)? How's your digestive system working?

- Get rid of all the junk food in your kitchen and purchase only healthy food with fills you with energy.

- Evaluate what blocks your energy. Look at your emotional well-being. Where can you strengthen it and improve?

- Incorporate into your schedule work with healing practitioners who support you. You may work with an acupuncturist, naturopath, chiropractor, shamanic drummer, chanter, chakra healer, meditation coach, and so forth.

- Check your bank balances daily. Reconcile your bank accounts.
- Know your personal boundaries and honor them!
- Do you have boundaries which work for you?
- How often to you allow others to trample them?
- What's non-negotiable in your life?
- Ask for the help you need!

Allowing What Is

"What if we let whatever is bothering us to just be, not judging it as good or bad? It just is."

– Lara Habig

When I glance back briefly over my life's journey, I can easily see behind me a string of disappointments. Suffering. Pain. Sadness. Lost love. I also see a string of wonderful surprises and blessings interwoven to make up my entire life's tapestry. Which one I choose to focus on determines how I feel at any given moment.

Sometimes, all I see and feel is what is happening in this moment. If I'm not careful, those unmet desires and disappointments could send me into a curled up ball, or even propel me to give up. I've given up to the disappointment many, many times. Sometimes, several times a day!

I don't understand why disappointment has to be a part of life. Why do children get cancer? Why are there car accidents? Why do people fight and kill? I do not know, but somehow, some way, I'm determined to stop fighting the disappointments in my life and learn from them.

To be disappointed means to be discouraged by the failure of one's hopes or expectations. When you're feeling down about a recent expectation or failed hope, life can seem awfully dismal. Hope gives you something to look forward to, to believe in, even trust. When that hope is shattered and the shards are everywhere, the question is, what now?

A little spark of hope inside was the only thing that kept me going on some days. It felt like that was all I had. On numerous occasions, my spark felt doused and no embers remained. The key word here is FEEL/FELT. I have a friend who says feelings are like farts... they come and go quickly! Something we need to remember this when we are having an emotional moment.

What happens when someone lets us down? What happens when we lose our hope? Or expectations aren't met? If you are like me, you throw things around and scream for a while! Just kidding, but I bet it would feel good. As I move through difficult times, I look back see a clearer reflection of my journey—all of it, the pain, and the pleasure. The sadness and the joy.

My whole experience makes up who I am today. Without one, the other can't exist. It's in the middle of the opposites that I try to reside. Centered, balanced, focused, not being attached to either/or. Just being. What if we let whatever is bothering us to just be, and didn't judge it as good or bad? It just is. How would that feel? What would happen if we didn't react to the drama playing out around us? We allowed it to be.

By answering these simple, yet complex questions, as difficult moments greet us, you will bring Your Soul's Calling to the forefront. You will no longer be able to deny the true you. You will know who you are and why you are here on earth. You will allow what is to be. You will KNOW you are ENOUGH. You will no longer judge yourself or others. Instead, you'll embrace the perfect moment as it is, no matter the emotion it produces.

It's important to:

- Recognize when we are adding to the drama.
- Notice what is happening around us and inside of us.
- Live in the moment.
- Recognize resistance or fear, and feel it.
- Allow what is to be and not judge it as good or bad.

Lately, I seem to have to answer these questions almost daily. My roller coaster life challenges and new business have pushed me to pursue my soul's calling on a level I can hardly comprehend. This book almost didn't get written. The fear inside of me about showing the world whom I truly am, almost won. The resistance I felt to finishing this project nearly caused me to give up. Because I've been there before, it was easy to recognize the pattern.

On the morning I was finishing this chapter, a fear overtook me that I can't explain. Of course, instead of writing, I read emails. In God's perfect timing, Dr. Christiane Northrup's email newsletter came through with these words of wisdom:

> *To birth something new, whether that's a baby, a book, a seminar or talk, a new relationship, or a new career, you have to have courage and faith. You also have to be ready to embrace change. Change is tough for many. As humans, we really want things to stay the same. We're creatures of habit—and so am I—even for small things. You may not be aware of this, but it's possible to give birth in an orgasmic way. Believe it or not, the energy that gets*

the baby in gets the baby out. And that's true biological-
ly, but it's also true in your personal life. To tap into this
incredible and powerful energy, you'll want to learn to
'surf with' change. When you feel resistance to change,
be present with it. Grieve for what's no longer going to be
there. That's the only way to usher all the good stuff in.
You have to feel it and move forward to give birth to the
new thing. Remember that when the good stuff comes
in, it brings in joy. And joy can flush out the loneliness,
the fear, and the other 'stuff' that is no longer serving
you. I have stood by while hundreds of women gave birth
to beautiful, normal babies. Just before the time to start
pushing came, nearly every woman would say, 'I can't
do this! I can't do this! I don't know how to do this!' And,
suddenly, there was a beautiful baby. While she didn't
know how to do it with her intellect, her body, and nature
knew just what to do. You know how to do it, too. And
your intellect may be the last thing to catch on. Have
faith. Have courage. Keep breathing. And simply know
that you're programmed for new beginnings.

Dr. Northrup's statement, "I can't do this! I can't do this! I don't know how to do this!" replayed over and over in my head. That's when I combined my own advice with Dr. Northrup's encouragement, got still, and began to recognize and notice what was happening for me. I stopped verbally abusing myself for feeling the way I did. I honored what was happening, and allowed it to just be. Then, I had to make a decision. Was I going to hide the rest of my life and deny the world my gift OR was I going to finish this book and live out my soul's calling? Obviously, I chose the latter!

Now it's your turn

Allowing What Is

When we fight against or judge the forces in our lives, we ultimately become stuck. Practicing mindfulness will support you as you:

- Recognize when you're adding to life's drama

- Notice what's going on inside and outside of you

- Live in the moment

- Recognize fear and resistance, leaning into the feelings, without judgment

- Allow what is to just be, judgment-free

- Choose your own path, forgive yourself (and others)

- Let go!

What Is Your Soul's Calling?

*"What in your life is calling you? When all the
noise is silenced, the meetings adjourned, the lists
laid aside, and the wild iris blooms by itself in
the dark forest, what still pulls on your soul?"*

– Terma Collective

Congratulations! You've made it to the end of this book! And, that my friend, is no small feat in today's busy world. You stepped up to the challenge to investigate your limitless soul, tapped into that spark inside of you, and allowed Your Soul's Calling to be revealed. You love yourself and KNOW you are ENOUGH. What a beautiful gift you have given yourself and those in your world.

As you journey through these practices in more detail, you can dive deeper, allowing Your Soul's Calling to shine brighter. In your stillness, you become present in the moment, reconnecting to God inside of you. This also gives buried feelings from long ago an opportunity to surface and be healed. Acknowledging your mind chatter produces an opening to choose your beliefs and quite possibly send you on a totally new, positive life-path trajectory. Practicing consistent Mindfulness and Meditation permits you to look at your life from a new perspective, providing clearer messages, increased energy, and reduced stress. Repeatedly, studies have shown that hanging out in nature can lower blood pressure, reduce anxiety, relieve stress, sharpen mental states, and even help those suffering from ADHD disorders, depression, addictions, insomnia, stress and more. Nature soothes, heals, restores, and connects us. Chaos turns to organization when you implement the proper Sleep, Schedules, and Surroundings for your life. Daily duties enjoy a smooth flow. To Rock What You've Got will remind you are ENOUGH.

When you Make Friends with Your Kitchen and embrace a healthy relationship with nourishing your body, you will begin to see the mask of low self-esteem melt away and heal the disconnection between your mind, body and soul. Your energy will increase and an overall quality of life will begin to take hold.

As you start feeling better about yourself, you naturally want to be around others. Your tribe will challenge you to be your best YOU, while loving and supporting you. In the Take Charge chapter, I challenged you to assume responsibility for your life, health, finances, boundaries, and self-love practices. By accepting this challenge, you will create a solid core of strength that will keep you steady as the world tilts around you. Last, but certainly not least, as you *Allow What Is*, you step away from drama to live in the moment. Judgement, fear, and resistance fade away when you notice the details.

As I mentioned earlier, I couldn't say the words self- love, but I knew in my heart that I needed to implement the loving practices outlined in this book. God led me step-by-step at my own pace in order to solidify each practice. The outcome has been a remarkable transformation from the inside, out. My life became aligned with my soul's purpose, allowing incredible joy and happiness to embody all that I am. Self-limiting beliefs that held me back disappeared. I began to value and love myself for the first time ever. I know now that I am ENOUGH. I am healthier in my mind, body and spirit. I have tools to work through resistance and fear. You, too, can expect the same results as you implement loving yourself practices.

You have learned you are in charge of creating your own your life. Take the pain, suffering, joy, all of it from the past, work through the practices outlined in this book, and allow your own spark or soul to speak to you. Allow Your Soul's Calling to reveal itself as your truest dreams come to life.

Aside from working through the steps outlined and actually getting this book finished, another dream come true for me was choosing to go on an impromptu trip out of the country for a weekend. A friend offered me free last minute tickets to a meet and greet and Def Leppard concert in Canada.

My mind chatter was telling me, "This is stupid. No one travels that far for a concert. This is silly. You have a hundred things to do so you should stay home and play it safe."

But inside I KNEW I needed to go. I love an adventure, especially when traveling to a place I've never visited before with a group of new friends. They were awesome, by the way!)

While watching the concert (from the third row), I realized the deep joy I felt because the band members of Def Leppard chose to do something they LOVE. They followed their own joy and were acting on their gifts, offering to the world their creativeness and all that they are. Not everyone in the world loves their music; however, there is a group of people with whom their gifts resonate and they want to hear more. Here's a truth: it's that way for all of us. When we are truly operating at our highest expression of who God created us to be, following our soul's calling, we are offering the world our own gift. We radiate immense joy to those around us which spreads like a wildfire. Not everyone is going to understand your message, or get Your Soul's Calling, but those who do will feel incredible joy and bliss from your gift that you offer them.

You are ENOUGH, today, in this moment. When healed, see your past pain and suffering as the conduit to your greatest gift to the world – Your Soul's Calling. Don't delay in loving and valuing yourself. The world is waiting for YOU!

Frequently Asked Questions

I lead a busy life—mother, grandmother, wife, work, and other activities. I am constantly exhausted trying to catch up with my life on the weekends but it never happens. What can I do to feel more peace and be more centered in my life?

My number one recommendation is to slow down. Cut out unnecessary activities in your life. Really look at how you are spending your time. Does it nourish you? Does it add to your life or deplete energy from you? As you begin to cut away unnecessary activities, use that time to sit and *Be Still*. Relax on your couch. Take extra time sipping that morning coffee and watching the birds play outside the window. Focus on enjoying the moment you are in. This simple, deliberate act of *Being Still* became a daily ritual that I relish even today. In the stillness, I began to be present, enjoy moments at a deeper level, feel feelings, release frustrations, reconnected to God, trust and honor myself, know that I was enough, hear God more clearly, and feel centered and energized to fulfill my soul's purpose. Without *Being Still,* we stumble through the noise. Without *Being Still* we take guesses at where we should be next. Without *Being Still* we don't honor our self or our true calling.

I constantly hear a lot of mind chatter. How do I know what's real? What's true? Or, what to believe?

It's human nature to have many different voices going on in our minds, sometimes all at once! The key is deciphering what to *listen* to. I've heard it explained that our mind chatter is like a channel on a radio station. We get to choose if we want to listen to a particular station (negative, self-defeating thoughts) or change the channel to a softer, more encouraging, loving channel. My best advice with mind chatter is if it makes you feel joyful and loving, pursue those thoughts. If the chatter makes you feel depleted, sad, depressed or angry, change that channel to one that lifts you up.

What's the best way to lower my daily stress?

I recommend specific breathing techniques, *Mindfulness and Meditation* as the fastest, least expensive, and most comprehensive way to lower the stress in your life. These three non-negotiable techniques need to be a part of your daily life to help diffuse the constant battering we do to ourselves. Regardless of the route, make adding these to your routine allows you to live in peace within yourself.

I understand that being in nature is beneficial to me, but I don't have the time it takes to find nature and not sure if it's really worth the effort.

I totally understand and agree with you. What I found and I think you will too, is the benefits far outweigh the effort it takes to breathe fresh air and explore natural landscapes. Spending time outdoors, whether resting, walking or hiking, helped reset my body when I felt uneasy, stressed, or unbalanced. The good news is just thinking about nature or looking at nature has almost the same effect as immersing yourself in it. Being outside provided many benefits for me personally and can for you as well. It helped me to mend my broken heart, release the past and old worn out patterns, and reconnect to myself and God.

I struggle with keeping to a schedule. Is it really important?

YES! Keeping a schedule that supports your life, your interests, and your family can catapult you to success beyond your wildest dreams. Your schedule is like a boat's rudder, it keeps your sailing toward your goals despite the choppy waters of daily stress. The best thing we can do is to honor our own personal rhythms regularly as we ride the waves of life. Scheduling a balance of quality sleep, work, play, relationship connection, healthy meals, and workouts every day sets you up to skyrocket your self-worth and self-love. Life is about living, loving and relationships. Schedules make certain the important people and activities in your life are a priority while the nonessentials fall away. That being said, we should be flexible with the changes the day brings while not being attached to our schedules.

My closet is a source of great pain. I run in and out of it as fast as I can. I even have beautiful clothes, but I do not wear them. I stick with black yoga pants and sweatshirts on most days. HELP!

Dressing is an act of self-love. If you're struggling in your closet and especially putting beautiful clothes on your body, you may be suffering from low self-esteem and lack of self-love. Low self-esteem shows up perfectly in how we dress (or not). If we don't feel good about ourselves, we may choose to not even show up for our life. Hence, the yoga pants as a daily uniform! Healthy self- esteem allows us to know we are enough in this moment. I encourage you to appreciate who you are, as you are. Look in the mirror when you get dressed and tell yourself, *Rock What You've Got*. Know you are ENOUGH. Right here. Right now. You don't have to be someone you are not. Be the best version of YOU. *Rock What You've Got* is about accepting and loving the body and your whole self in this moment. And, when you love who you are in this moment, you naturally begin to dress to reflect that beautiful inner you and feel rockin'.

In the chapter *Making Friends with Your Kitchen*, you talk a lot about proper nutrition and how you transformed your own body by changing the food you ate. What are some of your personal favorite meals?

Glad you asked! I love to begin my day with hot lemon water sweetened with a touch of honey. Breakfast on most days is brown organic eggs and olive oil cooked with greens and other veggies. In between breakfast and lunch, I enjoy a cup of green tea or Tee-cino, an organic decaf coffee alternative. Lunch may be a salad with more mixed veggies, sliced avocado and grilled chicken OR a smoothie with protein powder, a cup of berries, greens, and olive oil. Dinner is usually light—grilled salmon with veggies with baked sweet potato fries OR a Chipotle-like chicken Mexican bowl that I call my "Bowl of Awesomeness," made with lime, brown rice, chicken, avocado, and whatever veggies I have in the fridge.

My snacks are normally organic Gala apples, cottage cheese with cinnamon, cashews, almonds, homemade kale chips, or homemade chia seed pudding. Once a week, I splurge and make a homemade cafe latte with organic espresso, almond milk, honey and cinnamon. Because I have thyroid issues, my kale and other cruciferous veggies (broccoli, cauliflower, cabbage, Brussels sprouts and collard greens) are eaten cooked, not in smoothies. I try to keep my food clean, low carb, and organic. I'm not always perfect, but do my best each day. Himalayan Pink Salt and Bragg's Organic Seasoning are my spices of choice!

I am an introvert. Why do I need to be around people?

I'm asked this question often. Usually, it's in the context of, "I'm introspective and would rather be by myself than around others. Why should I reach out?" Humans by design are made to be in community. Studies have proven over and over that sick people get well not because of medicine, but because of their community and support systems. We need each other, and not only when we are sick. Even introverts benefit from being around a like-minded group of folks who can support them. If you are one who likes to be alone and focused inward, that's great. Do not change who you are! But instead, be open to the possibility of adding a few folks who have similar interests as you. Begin expanding your tribe (love and support) and benefit from the increased nourishment that it brings. The African proverb says, "If you want to go fast, go alone. If you want to go far, go together." Being a part of a tribe will allow you to feel loved and supported. It will also challenge you to grow into the best version of you. Take responsibility now for who you are, your values, and beliefs and watch your tribe expand!

As a people-pleaser, I don't want to disappoint people. I want to say YES to everyone who asks me to help. HELP!

None of us want to purposely disappoint others. If you are empathic or sensitive it can be downright devastating for you to say

NO to others. Honestly, though, if you do not set your boundaries, you're not doing anyone any favors. You will run yourself (health, life, family) into the ground so fast that you will be useless. Set your limits and make yourself a priority. This is loving yourself and your family. Examine what boundaries you have set in your life. Do you have definite boundaries placed around certain areas that are non-negotiable? And, even with those in place, we still need to be flexible for the true emergencies that pop up. Life is full of give and take moments. Even though I have a set schedule, I'm still very open to where or what God is leading me to do. Please take this advice from someone who is still struggling with health issues because of saying "yes" too often. Know you are ENOUGH and you do not have to earn your way or prove you are valuable. You are enough, right here and now.

My life is not playing out at all how I thought it'd be. How do I live with disappointment and shattered dreams?

I don't understand why disappointment or shattered dreams have to be a part of life. But I do believe with all my heart that we can learn to thrive among the hills and valleys of life. By following the advice in this book, you can overcome challenges from a higher place of love. Next time you are feeling that disappointment of dashed dreams, focus on allowing it to be in your life. Welcome it. Accept it. It's there anyway. May as well stop fighting it! Don't judge it. Let whatever is bothering you just *be*. This will help keep you centered and balanced, and not attached to either/or. You will be able to stay constant, steady, and strong, regardless of what swirls around you. You will be able to live from a place of action, not reaction. You can reside in the eye of the storm—calm and serene.

Final Thoughts

I'm not sure if you realize I wrote this book for you. You matter to me. You knowing deep down you are ENOUGH matters to me. I pray the stories and advice in *More Than Enough: Discover Your Limitless Potential and Live Your Bravest Dream* help you navigate your own adventures with confidence. Although this book has come to an end, you are at the beginning of your own personal journey to knowing you are ENOUGH. No longer can your past pain or suffering hold you back from your bravest dream. It can become the pathway to *Your Soul's Calling*, your life purpose. It all begins with loving yourself and knowing you are ENOUGH.

Please feel free to email me at LARA@LARAJAYE.COM anytime you feel called to reach out. I would be honored if you would share your success stories with me on how implementing the principles helped you or how I can better serve you.

Until then, always remember that you are *More Than Enough*.

About The Author

As an author, spiritual mentor, and speaker, Lara Jaye passionately inspires others to transformation. She teaches her clients how to shine light into their darkest corners, release stale patterns that keep them stuck, and discover their unique purpose. The outcome is unsurpassed clarity, confidence and connection. Not that long ago, she found herself swimming in denial and depression. Numbing herself with anti-depressants, she hid behind a mask of self-confidence while building her marketing company. Keeping up the charade only fueled her anxiety, eating disorders, and self-neglect.

A major health crisis, end of her 25-year marriage and a spiritual awakening brought Lara's "perfect" world to collapse. While viewing the pieces of what was her life, a voice whispered in her ear, "You are enough" and lit a spark of hope. Lara faced her demons, chose self-love over self-hate, and began her limitless journey.

Lara works with those individuals who yearn to live a fuller, purposeful life, where money and worldly possessions no longer satisfy. She offers an array of services, including 1:1 mentoring, VIP Days, group retreats, online classes, workshops and speaking.

For more information, please visit www.LaraJaye.com.

Download Your Free Gift

Are you reluctant to trust yourself?

Do you struggle with anger, frustration or depression?

Is it hard for you to accept compliments?

If you said "YES!" to any of the questions above, then be sure to download your FREE BONUS GIFT -- *Loving Yourself Just For Today*, a colorful printable poster that you can post anywhere in your home or office. It can also be used as wallpaper for your phone or computer.

This poster, packed with self-love practices, will act as a reminder to take care of yourself in the midst of your hectic daily life. Each day as you implement one or several of the suggestions, the effects will be cumulative, allowing your confidence to soar. You will essentially begin to see yourself as worthy, valuable, and belonging in the world, deserving of happiness. And, most importantly, a belief will emerge that you are ENOUGH, as you are in this moment.

DOWNLOAD YOUR FREE
BONUS GIFT TODAY:

www.LaraJaye.com/BookOffer